CW01669206

Leadership Challenge

The Complete Guide to Master your Leadership Skills. Principles and Practical Habits to Start the Change. Increase your Grit and Self Confidence with Emotional Intelligence

By

Maxwell Cooper

© Copyright 2019 - All rights reserved.

The content contained within this book may not be reproduced, duplicated or transmitted without direct written permission from the author or the publisher.
Under no circumstances will any blame or legal responsibility be held against the publisher, or author, for any damages, reparation, or monetary loss due to the information contained within this book. Either directly or indirectly.

Legal Notice:

This book is copyright protected. This book is only for personal use. You cannot amend, distribute, sell, use, quote or paraphrase any part, or the content within this book, without the consent of the author or publisher.

Disclaimer Notice:

Please note the information contained within this document is for educational and entertainment purposes only. All effort has been executed to present accurate, up to date, and reliable, complete information. No warranties of any kind are declared or implied. Readers acknowledge that the author is not engaging in the rendering of legal, financial, medical or professional advice. The content within this book has been derived from various sources. Please consult a licensed professional before attempting any techniques outlined in this book.
By reading this document, the reader agrees that under no circumstances is the author responsible for any losses, direct or indirect, which are incurred as a result of the use of information contained within this document, including, but not limited to, — errors, omissions, or inaccuracies.

Table of Contents

Introduction

We've all heard the term "emotional intelligence," but what does that really mean? Is it really as important as experts claim? Is EQ really just as important as IQ in the workplace? Better yet, how can you increase my emotional intelligence to improve your leadershipskills?

Emotional Intelligence for Leadership is an invaluable resource, and it will guide you through the answers to these questions and many more. By the time you've finished reading this book, you'll understand the importance of emotional intelligence and learn how to integrate it (and other skills) into your successful leadership style.

There are five fundamental tenets of emotional intelligence (self-awareness, self-regulation, motivation, empathy, and social skills). Emotional Intelligence for Leadership explores each facet, in depth, so that you can comprehend it and apply the understanding to increasing your own emotional intelligence.

Emotional intelligence is part of every aspect of our lives, from intimate relationships to workplace leadership. It's important to learn strategies and skills to enhance your understanding of your own emotions, and therefore the emotions of others. Whether it's deciding body language or identifying a behavioral communication style, you will equip yourself with the tools necessary for finding success in all areas of your life.

If you're wondering if emotional intelligence is different for men and women, you're not alone. *Emotional Intelligence for Leadership* breaks down the neurobiological differences between males and females so that you can better understand why someone else's brain might operate a little differently than yours.

Examining your own emotions, and discovering the valuable purpose they serve, is the first step to increasing your emotional intelligence. *Emotional Intelligence for Leadership* gives you practical advice about how to improve your active listening skills, how to manage your negative emotions, and how to read body language and other nonverbal cues. What's more, this book will outline how to successfully incorporate emotional intelligence into your cognition so that your logical decision making is as comprehensive as possible.

Leadership Challenge guides you through what it means to be truly resilient and how to turn adversities in your life into a success story. If you need the motivation to make changes, you want to learn what leadership competencies are, or you want to learn how to communicate in a clear, positive way, *Leadership Challenge* is the book for you.

Learn the secrets to utilizing your emotional intelligence and other strengths to make the transition from a team member to a leadership position. Find out the most common mistakes leaders make, so that you don'thave to.

Emotional Intelligence for Leadership is a comprehensive guide that not only informs you about psychological research, but also teaches you to apply the knowledge to your own skill set so that you're able to achieve success. Read Emotional Intelligence for Leadership, fine-tune your communication skills, and begin your journey into leadership.

Chapter 1:

What is Emotional Intelligence?

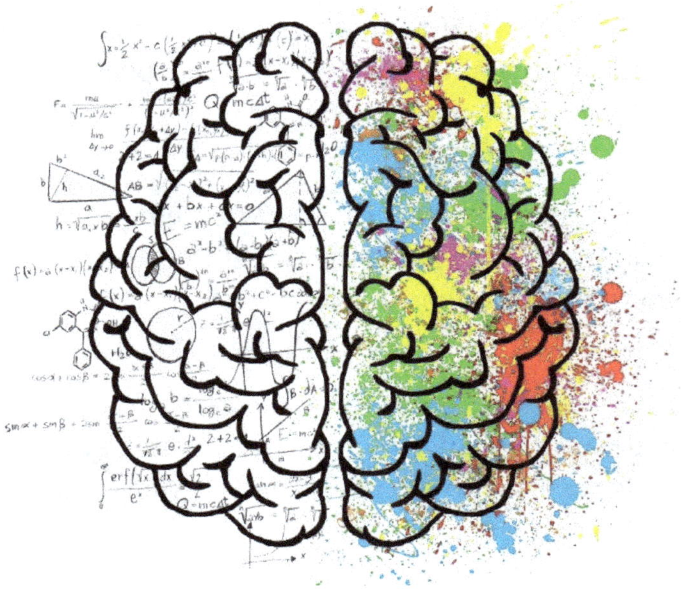

Emotional intelligence is your ability to not only self- monitor your emotions, but also observe the emotions of people around you. It includes your capacity to identify various emotions and accurately label them. The ability to articulate how you're feeling serves as a guide; you're able to synthesize the information about your emotions. The way you think and behave reflects this.

Thinking, decision making, and understanding are improved when you combine emotions and empathy with your intelligence. This blend enhances how you appreciate and comprehend the dynamics of how you relate to others.

High emotional intelligence is linked to the following:

- Interpersonal skills. Having emotional intelligence means that you socially interact well with others and form relationships. It also indicates that you are likely to adhere to social norms and not exhibit antisocial behavior. Relationships with family and partners come naturally.
- Likability. If you have high emotional intelligence, others tend to see you as amiable, empathetic, and socially adept. Your emotional intelligence makes people want to be around you.
- Scholastic achievement. Emotional intelligence helps you achieve more in academics.
- Self-awareness. If you are emotionally intelligent, you understand yourself. Additionally, your choices are based on a combination of emotion and logic.
- Self-esteem. High emotional intelligence corresponds with low insecurity levels. It means that you care about your well-being, mentallyand otherwise.
- Positive workplace dynamics. Having the ability to relate to others leads to favorable work performance.

If you're conscious of your own emotions, and you're able to recognize and acknowledge the feelings that others have, it greatly benefits the relationships you have. You're able to see various perspectives, empathize with others, and make valuable connections. High emotional intelligence is beneficial to your own well- being, as well as the well-being of those around you.

Ability Model, Mixed Model, and Trait Model

There are three different emotional intelligence models: the ability model, the mixed model, and the trait model. Having three separate models promoted the need for different ways to assess emotional intelligence. There is a bit of overlap, but the measures typically calculate differently.

Ability models focus on the various ways emotions aid our thinking and understanding. Depending on the context, it might be appropriate for you to either involve or eliminate emotions from your thought process. Including emotion and having it interact with your intellect can improve your decision-making skills.

Emotional intelligence doesn't have one simple definition; rather, it's a construct that embodies several things:

- ability to perceive your (and others') emotions
- ability to help your thought process by accessing and producing emotions
- ability to think about your emotions
- ability to enhance your thinking by recognizing emotions
- ability to comprehend emotional knowledge
- ability to self-regulate your emotions

The Ability Model

The ability model considers emotions to be valuable sources of data that help us navigate our environment. It states that we all have varying abilities when it comes to applying the emotional information to our thinking as a whole. The ability shows itself through different behaviors. The ability model asserts that emotional intelligence consists of four different abilities.

1. Managing your emotions. If you have emotional intelligence, you have the ability to harness your feelings and manage them.
2. Perceiving emotions. If you're emotionally intelligent, you have the ability to sense others' emotions through things like facial expressions and voices. This ability is essentially the front lines of your emotional intelligence; once you're ableto detect someone's feelings, your brain can process the emotional information.
3. Understanding emotions. Recognizing and describing the nuances among different feelings are abilities that indicate you understand emotions. Some emotions can be complex, and it is a valuable skill to be able to appreciate their dynamics.
4. Using emotions. An emotionally intelligent person is able to think and problem-solve while incorporating his or her emotions. If you have the ability to use your emotions, you can capitalizeon your own range of moods.

Psychologists John D. Mayer, Peter Salovey, and David R. Caruso developed the Mayer-Salovey-Caruso Emotional Intelligence Test (MSCEIT). It is designed to assess a person's emotional intelligence by measuring how well he or she is able to solve problems, react to social situations, and interpret facial expressions. The evaluation tests a person's abilities in the four areas of the ability model: managing, perceiving, understanding, and using emotion. The participant receives a score for each of these four components.

Since the four-branch ability model is predicated on the idea that emotional intelligence is aligned with social norms, a participant's answers on the MSCEIT are compared to those supplied by a multitude of respondents. The score is therefore calculated in aconsensus manner. Alternatively, answers can be compared to those of a group of 21 professional researchers. There are no objectively correct answers.

The Mixed Model

The mixed model, designed by Daniel Goleman, asserts that emotional intelligence consists of numerous skills and competencies that contribute to leadership performance. The mixed model shows five primary tenets of emotional intelligence.

1. Empathy. This involves recognizing and considering others' feelings.
2. Motivation. This refers to your ambition and drive to succeed.
3. Self-awareness. This is the ability to know your own strengths, weaknesses, and emotions, while also

recognizing the effect you have on others.

4. Self-regulation. This includes the ways you control or redirect any disruptive emotions. It also refers to the way you adapt to change.
5. Social skills. This refers to the way you're able to manage various relationships.

It's important to remember that emotional capabilities are not innate traits; rather, they are learned skills that require growth and development. Goleman asserts that we are all born with a general emotional intelligence with certain potential for ability.

There are two tools for measuring emotional intelligence using the mixed model. In 1999, the Emotional Competency Inventory (ECI) was developed. It was updated in 2007 and renamed the Emotional and Social Competency Inventory (ESCI). It is designed to provide a measurement of a person's competency (in both emotional and social frameworks). In addition, the Emotional Intelligence Appraisal was developed in 2001. It can be a self-reporting or 360-degree assessment.

Trait Model

The trait model, developed by Konstantinos V. Petrides, is your own self-perceptions of your emotional capabilities. Conceptually, it's different from the ability model, and the measurement comes from your own self- reported answers. The trait model definition of emotional intelligence includes both behavioral dispositions and emotional capabilities that you gauge and report for yourself. This model is not concerned with actual ability; it focuses on emotional self-efficacy.

The trait model actually includes the mixed model. If we look at emotional intelligence as a personality trait, the concept is more than just cognitive ability. This is the biggest distinction between the trait model and the ability model.

Self-reporting assessments in the trait model, such as the Schutte EI model, EQ-i, and the Swinburne University Emotional Intelligence Test (SUEIT), do not measure capability, skill, or intelligence. They simply measure trait emotional intelligence. Of the assessments, the EQ-i 2.0 is the most widely used. It is available in multiple languages, and it has the best validity, reliability, and norms.

The Bottom Line

As you can see, there isn't one concise definition of emotional intelligence. Instead, it's a concept that subsumes multiple factors. To have high emotional intelligence means that you understand your emotions, and you utilize a substantial vocabulary to describe your feelings. Someone might say that he or she feels "bad," but am emotionally intelligent person can identify a more precise description of his or her feelings. The emotionally intelligent person might say that he or she feels resentful, frustrated, or apologetic.

Chapter 2:

The History of Emotional Intelligence

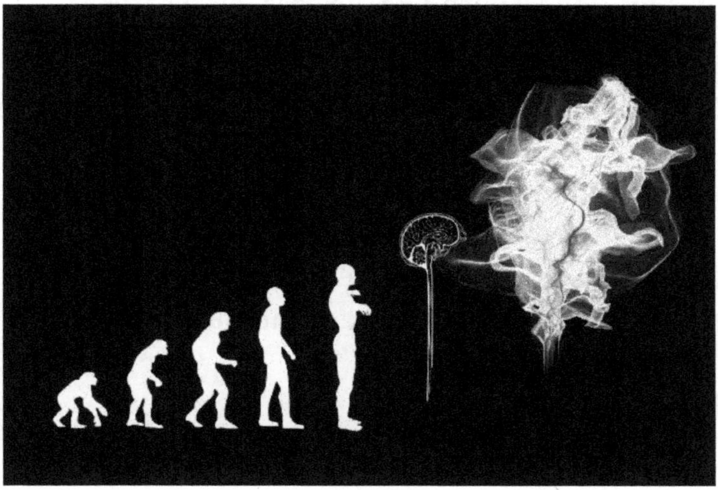

The concept of emotional intelligence has been explored since the 1930s. Over time, research has led psychologists to expand the discipline. It has evolved into what we now know as the branch of social psychology known as emotional intelligence.

1930s

Edward Lee Thorndike, a psychologist and professor at Columbia University, focused on comparative psychology. His work with the learning process evolved into the theory of connectionism; he was fundamental in the beginning stages of the study of educational psychology.

Thorndike, who was the American Psychological Association's president in 1912, developed exams for employees in the workplace. As a board member with the Psychological Corporation, Thorndike devises employment assessments for the military and civilian employers.

In the 1930s, Thorndike differentiated three primary areas of intellectual development. Abstract intelligence refers to the ability to understand and process various concepts. Mechanical intelligence is a person's ability to handle and manipulate tangible objects. Social intelligence, a term coined by Thorndike, refers to the ability to navigate human interaction.

1940s

David Wechsler, a Romanian psychologist, was one of the earliest supporters of including social aptitude in psychological testing. While he didn't directly assess non-intellective factors, he asserted that they affected intelligent behavior and needed to be considered. He was the first to suggest that social factors, and the way they impact a person's intelligence, could be necessary for finding success in life.

Before David Wechsler began developing his own intelligence assessments, the Binet scale (created in 1937) was used. Wechsler disagreed with the linear approach and single score offered by the Binet, so in 1939, he developed the Wechsler Adult Intelligence Scale (WAIS). It was later called the Wechsler-Bellevue Intelligence Test, and derivations of that included the Wechsler Intelligence Scale for Children (WISC) and the Wechsler Preschool and Primary Scale of Intelligence (WPPSI), in 1949 and 1967, respectively.

Wechsler's assessments were initially designed to glean information about his patients. His evaluations are still predicated on the concept that intelligence is about more than just rational thought. His philosophy was that a person's ability to competently navigate his or her environment is an essential component of intelligence.

1950s

Abraham Maslow, famous for his hierarchy of needs, was one of the first psychologists to spotlight happy people and their psychological paths. Rather than focus on the negative aspects of patients'

psychological profiles, Maslow chose to make people's

self-fulfillment an integral part of his work.

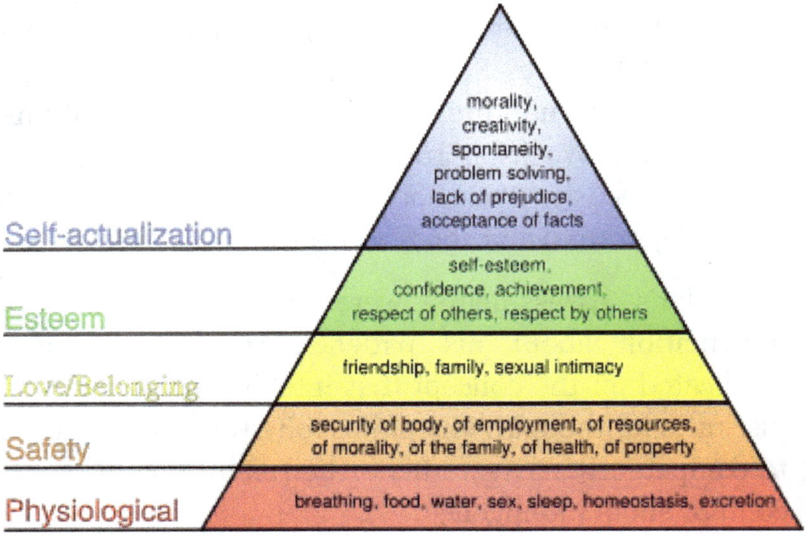

morality,
creativity,
spontaneity,
problem solving,
lack of prejudice,
acceptance of facts
Self-actualization
self-esteem,
confidence, achievement,
respect of others, respect by others
Esteem
friendship, family, sexual intimacy
Love/Belonging
security of body, of employment, of resources,
of morality, of the family, of health, of property
Safety
breathing, food, water, sex, sleep, homeostasis, excretion
Physiological

Maslow examined healthy people to try to understand humans' capabilities. He looked at historical leaders and their motivations to get a better grasp on human potential. His focus was on history's best and brightest in the context of their societies in order to conclude the extent of human potential.

Maslow asserted that people who are self-actualized tend to lead lives with a greater sense of well-being and fulfillment. This stems from their accurate perception of reality. According to Maslow, self-actualized people:

- show gratitude for their lives
- are not self-centered
- focus on solving problems
- think independently
- are not excessively influenced by others
- have a sense of kinship with all humans
- have a philosophical sense of humor

Abraham Maslow, along with his fellow humanistic psychologists, detailed how we can build our own emotional strength. Before the 1950s, developing emotional durability was not a consideration.

1975

Howard Gardner, a now-retired professor at Harvard University's Graduate School of Education, is a developmental psychologist whose work has become an integral component in educational psychology. In 1975, Gardner published *The Shattered Mind,* which introduced us to his theory of multiple intelligences.

According to Gardner, we have various independent ways to process information. Traditionally, IQ tests had accounted for logical, linguistic, and spatial abilities. Gardner's theory asserted that a person's abilities are not limited to these three areas; additionally, they're not necessarily correlated. Multiple intelligences meant that a person's interpersonal and intrapersonal skills now had their own measurements.

1983

Howard Gardner published Frames of Mind: The Theory of Multiple Intelligences in 1983. It detailed his theory that intelligence, in a traditional sense, was not sufficient in explaining a person's ability. Gardner explained the importance of including interpersonal intelligence (a person's ability to comprehend others' motivations and desires) and intrapersonal intelligences (a person's ability to understand things such as his or her own motivations, fears, and feelings).

1985

In his 1985 doctoral dissertation, "A study of emotion: developing emotional intelligence; self-integration; relating to fear, pain and desire (theory, structure of reality, problem-solving, contraction/expansion, tuning in/coming out/letting go)," Wayne Payne proposed the concept of emotional intelligence.

1987

In 1987, Keith Beasley used the phrase "emotional quotient" in a *Mensa Magazine* article. It is believed to be the first time this term was published; however, Reuven Bar-On asserts that he used "emotional quotient" in his graduate thesis. Incidentally, the version of his thesis that contains the term was not published.

1989

Stanley Greenspan, a professor of psychiatry, behavioral science, and pediatrics at the George Washington University, was a pediatric psychiatrist whose work focused on children with disabilities. In 1989, he presented a model that described emotional intelligence.

1990

Peter Salovey and John Mayer are psychologists who published "Emotional Intelligence," an article in *Imagination, Cognition, and Personality,* in 1990. They stated that emotional intelligence is a skill set that allows us to:

- regulate our (and others') emotions
- express emotions
- use feelings to help us achieve success in life

The article, essentially a launching pad for the study of emotional intelligence, examined social ability and its role in the concept of overall intelligence. It provided a framework for incorporating emotional intelligence into mental health research and suggested areas that could possibly be explored to enhance the understanding thereof.

1995

In 1995, *New York Times* journalist Daniel Goleman published a book titled *Emotional Intelligence: Why It Can Matter More Than IQ*. It spent more than 18 months on the *New York Times* Best Seller list. Goleman explained how our two minds (both emotional and rational) cooperatively work to help us achieve. The conceptual idea of emotional intelligence became popular with the release of *Emotional Intelligence: Why It Can Matter More Than IQ*, and we began looking differently at what it means to be smart.

1998

Daniel Goleman published *Working with Emotional Intelligence* in 1998. It outlined how social skills can be just as important as cognitive skills for achieving success in the workplace. It served as a practical guide for us to discover how we can improve our emotional intelligence to reach our professional goals. It thoroughly explained that social skills are what set leaders apart from the general population.

1999

In 1999, Howard Gardner introduced us to the eight separate intelligences in his theory:

- bodily and kinesthetic
- interpersonal
- intrapersonal
- linguistic

- logical and mathematical
- musical
- naturalistic
- spatial

Gardner's theory of multiple intelligences has helped educators develop curriculum and instruction in ways that allow students to better comprehend material. It appeals to the idea that everyone has intelligence; it's a matter of looking past the traditional definition that only included cognitive ability.

2001

Daniel Goleman, along with Richard Boyatzis and Annie McKee, published Primal Leadership: Unleashing the Power of Emotional Intelligence, in 2001. This book became an important tool for professional leaders, as they began to understand that being emotionally intelligent is a necessity if they were to achieve success.

2009

In 2009, Howard Gardner proposed that a ninth branch should be added to the list of multiple intelligences. He suggested that existential intelligence (including moral intelligence) should be added to the list of eight.

Chapter 3:
EQ vs. IQ

Intelligence quotient (IQ) and emotional quotient (EQ) both measure a person's abilities, but they measure very different things.

What is EQ?

Emotional intelligence, also known as emotional quotient (EQ), is a person's ability to manage his or her emotions by identifying, evaluating, controlling, and expressing them. If you have a high EQ, then chances are that you make both a good leader and a team player. It means that you are able to understand and connect with those around you.

EQ is your ability to incorporate emotions into your thoughts and reasoning. A person with a high EQ uses his or her feelings to facilitate his or her logical thought process. He or she is also able to manage emotions, recognize other people's feelings, and comprehend what emotions mean. Your EQ is determined in part by how well you're able to relate to other people while maintaining control over your emotions.

What is IQ?

Intelligence quotient (IQ) is a numeric score that is the result of standardized tests developed to evaluate a person's intelligence. The score is used to determine a person's capabilities in an academic setting, but it's also used to recognize any individuals who have either gifted intelligence or intellectual disabilities.

Your IQ score is directly connected to intellect. It reflects your ability to learn, understand, and apply information. It includes math skills, language comprehension, and logic. If you have a high IQ, you're able to think in an abstract fashion and apply critical thinking skills to make connections.

Evaluation and Measurement

It can be difficult to measure EQ, as the evaluation is subjective, but there are standardized tests that calculate a person's emotional intelligence into quantifiable data. Tests typically have both supporters and critics in the psychology community.

Daniel Goldman's assessment measures a person's emotional competency. It uses either the Emotional Intelligence Appraisal or the Emotional Competency Inventory. Participants report their own perceptions of their competencies. Alternatively, the Mayer-Salovey- Caruso Emotional Intelligence Test is comprised of questions that measure a person's problem-solving skills with situations that are emotion based. The score indicates a participant's ability to reason when there is a given set of emotional information.

EQ testing can be a valuable tool to predict a person's likely success in a career and the ability to work as part of a team. A person with a high EQ typically does quite well in the workplace. EQ is a reliable indicator of career success, and it can be used to identify candidates who will be good leaders. The subjective results make it extremely important to record answers that are as accurate as possible.

IQ testing, which has been in place longer than that of EQ, is intended to be objective. The first "true" IQ evaluation, the Stanford-Binet test, was the first assessment to take into account a participant's age. Scoring is calculated by dividing the participant's mental age (according to the test) by his or her chronological age, then multiplying by 100. For example, if a participant who is 27.5 years old has a mental age score of 30, his or her IQ would be 109.

David Wechsler designed three separate tests to measure IQ. One is for young children, the second is for older children, and the third is for adults. Each is divided into subtests, and each subtest is measured against norms for the participant's age.

The Woodcock-Johnson Test of Cognitive Abilities is another widely used IQ test. It thoroughly measures a broad range of a person's cognitive abilities.

There isn't one IQ test that is considered by psychologists to be the best; various assessments are utilized throughout the education setting. They are regularly used in schools. While supporters assert that the standardized nature of these tests ensures fair and objective scores, some types of questions can actually display bias against minorities.

IQ testing is a valuable tool when educators are determining the needs for a student who requires special education. They can also uncover a student's hidden talents. While IQ testing provides useful information, it only shows us part of the picture. An IQ test does not take into account a participant's originality or creativity; it only focuses on intellectual thinking. IQ assessments do not accurately predict success in school or at work, because they exclude any abilities that are not academic in nature.

Which is More Important?

Some people tend to disagree on the answer to this question. Those who assert that EQ is more valuable than IQ argue that a high IQ is helpful for school, but that's only one phase of life. A high EQ leads to sustained success throughout all phases of life, regardless of setting.

EQ vs. IQ

	EQ	IQ
Definition	Emotional quotient (or emotional intelligence) refers to a person's emotional abilities as they pertain to himself or herself and others	Intelligence quotient is a person's score from an intelligence assessment that is standardized
Abilities	recognizing and assessing others' feelings, incorporating emotion into thinking, understanding meanings of emotions, identifying / evaluating / controlling / expressing emotions	learning, understanding, application of information, reasoning, comprehension, math, spatial relations, abstract thought, filtering unnecessary information
Workplace	initiative, cooperation, relationships, service,	research and development, analysis, challenging

	leadership, teamwork	tasks, problem solving
Identifies	people with social challenges, people who work better alone, people who are team players, people who are leaders	people with intellectual disabilities or special needs, people who are gifted or highly capable
History	*In 1985, Wayne Payne published his thesis titled, "A Study of Emotion: Developing Emotional Intelligence." In 1995, Daniel Goleman published Emotional Intelligence: Why it CanMatter More than IQ.*	In 1883, Francis Galton wrote a statistics paper titled, Inquiries into Human Faculty and Its Development." In 1905, psychologist Alfred Binet assessed French schoolchildren's intelligence.
Assessments	Daniel Goleman model, Mayer-Salovey-Caruso Test	Wechsler, Woodcock-Johnson Tests of Cognitive Abilities, Stanford-Binet

Historically speaking, IQ has been the standard measure of a person's intelligence; however, there is a direct correlation between high EQ and success in his or her career. That person will achieve more, take initiative, and work well with others. Many large corporations require EQ testing during the hiring process, because scores are reliable indicators of candidates' potential success. Additionally, many companies offer guided courses on social and emotional skills, because they're a quality investment. Employees participating in Social and Emotional Learning (SEL) leads to overall success.

Chapter 4: Components of Emotional Intelligence

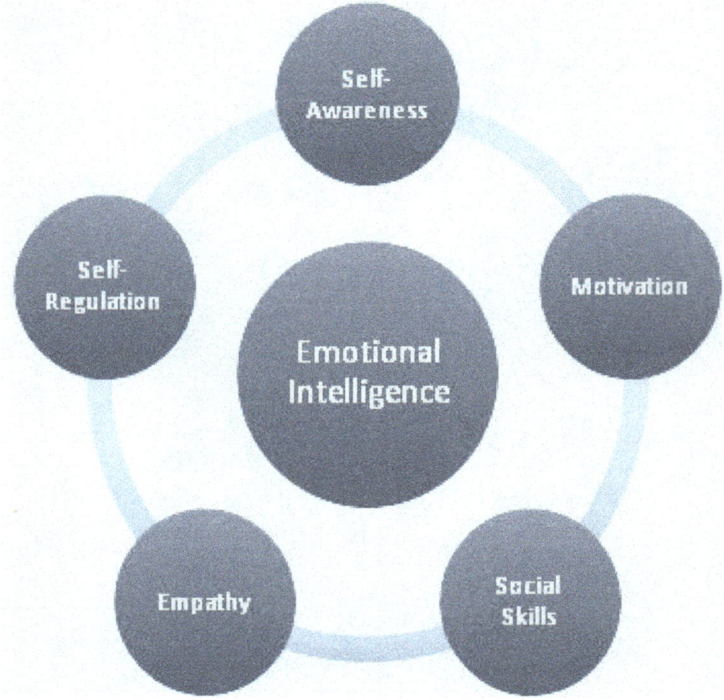

Intelligence is your ability to obtain information and acquire skills, then effectively and appropriately apply that new knowledge. Emotional intelligence, on the other hand, is your ability to successfully interact with others. Our emotions are essentially feelings, observable behaviors, and fluctuations in disposition. Your individual emotions help to form your unique perceptions. When we understand ourselves, we can better understand others. Daniel Goleman taught us that there are five integral components of emotional intelligence:

self-awareness
self-regulation
motivation
empathy social
skills

Self-Awareness

Self-awareness is your ability to identify and understand your abilities, strengths, weaknesses, moods, and motivations. To accomplish this, you need to be able to observe and audit your own emotional state, recognize your emotions, and identify them. Someone who is emotionally mature is confident; he or she is also aware of how other people perceive him or her. (This skill comes from being able to read another person's reactions.) Additionally, if you're an emotionally mature person, you're able to laugh at yourself and any mistakes you might make.

Your self-awareness is your ability to recognize yourself as an individual. It means that you're able to see yourself as a separate entity from your surroundings and other people. It's impossible to successfully build other emotional intelligence skills without having the foundation of self-awareness.

Self-awareness theory, developed in 1972, asserts that when we're introspective, we use our own values and standards to evaluate our behavior. When we are self- aware, we are more likely to align our behavior withour values.

When we're self-aware about our own cognition, there's overall improvement with reasoning, working memory, and processing efficiency. Additionally, your belief in your abilities lays the foundation for how you behave, feel, and think.

Self-Regulation

Self-regulation refers to your ability to appropriately express yourself while controlling any impulses and thinking before you speak. It means that even if someone else's emotions and behavior are illogical or incoherent, you're able to appropriately respond. Mastering self-regulation also entails taking accountability for your words and actions. Your emotional well-being depends on your ability to self- regulate.

In terms of behavior, self-regulating involves acting in a way that coordinates with your values. Having the ability to self-regulate means that your behavior aligns with your best interest in the long term. As it applies to emotion, self-regulation is your ability to do things like soothe your own feelings of anxiety, compose yourself when you're upset, and cheer yourself up when you're feeling sad.

Emotions are what drive us. In fact, the word "emotion" comes from the Latin "motus," which means "motion."

In ancient times, people said that their emotions moved their behavior. (Now, we say that they motivate it.) Our emotions signal chemical responses in our bodies, and all emotions have one of these motivations:

- Approach. Some examples of "approach" emotions are compassion, enjoyment, interest, love, and trust. "Approach" behaviors include things like cooperating, encouraging, guiding, learning, and protecting.

- Attack. Some examples of "attack" emotions are anger, contempt, disgust, and hatred. "Attack" behaviors include things like abusing, coercing, demanding, manipulating, and threatening.

- Avoid. Some examples of "avoid" behaviors are avoiding, dismissing, ignoring, rejecting, and withdrawing.

It can be challenging to self-regulate when you focus on feelings, because they can become magnified or skewed. It is easier to find success with self-regulation if you instead focus on your values. If you tell someone, "I feel angry," it highlights the feeling. This can lead to misinterpretation, but more importantly, it doesn't help resolve the issue. If you focus on what's wrong (the reasons you feel angry), it becomes easier to improve the situation. For example, saying, "The reason I feel angry is ...," the focus is on what needs to be resolved.

Motivation

Motivation refers to the interest you have in learning more and improving yourself. When life presents obstacles in your path, it's your motivation that keeps you strong enough to continue. If you're motivated, it means you set goals for yourself and you follow through on achieving them. An emotionally mature person has motivation that involves perseverance, commitment, and initiative.

To have high emotional intelligence, your initiative needs to include goals that are driven by internal motivation. These goals reflect your desire to improve yourself, rather than impress others.

Empathy

Empathy, understanding others' emotions, is impossible to achieve without first having self-awareness. To be able to understand other people, you must first be able to understand yourself. An emotionally mature person can show empathy toward others by understanding what society's norms are and why people behave the way we do. Additionally, an empathetic person is perceptive, interested in others' thoughts and concerns, and able to recognize a person's emotional response in the context of a specific situation.

When you are truly empathetic, it's because you understand your own emotions well enough to be able to see and feel how another person is feeling. Even if that person isn't similar to you, you recognize that we humans all feel emotions that cause us to react.

Empathy, which involves your ability to be a good leader and communicator by understanding other people's feelings, results in things such as:

- better health
- improved quality of life
- strong interpersonal relationships
- success in the workplace

Understanding others' thoughts and views involves being a good listener. Empathy also means others find you trustworthy. If you're empathetic, your friends likely speak openly with you, and your coworkers are likely to trust you. This trust leads to improved communication.

Social Skills

An emotionally mature person who has social skills is able to maintain relationships, find commonality with others, provide customer service, utilize sarcasm, and pick up on things like jokes and social cues. Additionally, it means having skills such as:

- communication
- problem solving
- negotiating
- time management
- leadership
- persuasion
- cooperation
- conflict management

An emotionally intelligent person is able to influence and manage others' emotions. Be careful not to confuse this with manipulation. Impacting other people's emotions can be something as basic as smiling or playing music, knowing that it leads others to feel more positive. It's important to be able to read others' emotions so that you can tweak your words and actions to best appeal to those people. If you're able to affect and excite others, you can win them over and persuade them to openly listen to your ideas.

Communication is an essential component of social skills. You must be able to listen to other people, of course, but you also must be able to clearly and accurately express your own feelings and thoughts. When you listen to someone, it's important to make sure you've clearly understood what has been communicated.

Managing conflicts, whether you're directly involved did or not, take skill. Disagreements occur all the time. Being able to manage conflicts is essential in all settings, especially the workplace. An emotionally intelligent person knows how to use tact to help resolve these situations.

Emotional intelligence is a component of leadership skills, but the inverse is also true. The two are undoubtedly connected. A good leader who is emotionally intelligent is able to clearly articulate ideas and positively influence others with them. It's important to remember that leadership is not exclusive to formal positions, and anyone can act as a leader. Additionally, a leader with solid social skills will guide and support coworkers or peers while also holding them accountable.

Social skills also include building rapport with others, your ability to cooperate and collaborate promotes an environment that causes others to want to do the same. Of the five components of emotional intelligence, your social skills are what are most obvious to others.

Chapter 5:
The Benefits of Emotional Intelligence at Work

Emotional intelligence can make a real difference in the workplace. Choices that we make, even in business, can be fueled by emotion. Following your "gut instinct" means that you're in tune with your emotions. Understanding where those emotions are coming from helps us connect and cooperate better with other members of our team.

I'm the 21st century, business is global. It's more important than ever to be emotionally intelligent, because the interactions we have with other people are complex. If you're working with people from various cultures, it is essential that you understand and accurately express your emotions. It makes a difference when it's time to solve problems under pressure.

When we're self-aware, we understand our own needs. We're also adept at anticipating reactions to events, and emotional intelligence allows us to explore alternate solutions. Emotional intelligence begins with you; it's impossible to enhance the well-being of others until you truly understand how your emotional self operates.

Leaders stand out because the skills that come with their emotional intelligence allow them to build a productive, efficient workplace. If you consider Daniel Goleman's tenets of emotional intelligence, you can see how valuable these traits are for employees.

- Self-awareness. It's essential to recognize and understand your own strengths and weaknesses. Self-awareness is also quite helpful when it's time to receive constructive feedback from others.

- Self-regulation. We all know that emotional outbursts at work are highly inappropriate, but self-regulation extends past that. If you are able to successfully self-regulate, it means that you utilize tact and diplomacy when expressing yourself and communicating with others.

- Motivation. If you're emotionally intelligent, your motivation is intrinsic. You work hard because you feel pride and fulfillment when you accomplish things. Self-driven people are extremely valuable in the workplace.

- Empathy. If you show empathy, you're more likely to have people trust you and follow your lead. It's important to understand how others feel and perceive the world; being open to others' perspectives makes collaborative work happen much more smoothly.
- Social skills. You want coworkers to trust you, and having a positive rapport is important. Think of

social skills as the act of putting the other four pillars to use. Emotional intelligent people with great social skills are able to show others that they're empathetic, self-aware, self-regulatory, and motivated.

Strategies for Using Emotional Intelligence at Work

Employees with emotional intelligence are an asset to any organization and tapping into that advantage can really help a company set itself apart from its competitors. There are three strategies that you can use that will help you maximize the benefits of emotional intelligence.

1. **Make emotional intelligence a priority.** It's not necessary - or even a good idea - to "turn off" your emotions when you go to work. For a business leader, it's important to approach situations with an emotionally intelligent perspective. Employees want to have a relationship that includes respect and trust; if they're not provided that, they'll find an employer who will give it to them. Emotional intelligence is correlated with good health - both physical and mental. If a leader utilized emotional intelligence to improve interpersonal relations at work, employees will most likely remain loyal and hardworking. Considering this, business leaders should seek emotionally intelligent people for hire and promotion. Additionally, it serves everyone if they also help to increase current employees' emotional intelligence. A successful professional has a balanced combination of work ethic, skill, and emotional intelligence.

2. **Foster an emotionally intelligent culture.** Emotional intelligence is a skill, and it's worth practicing. Organizations should develop an environment that is conducive to practicing the different tenets of emotional intelligence. This is important for everyone, including employees and managers. An organization can do thisby showing

employees that emotional intelligence is a core value. Employees should see that their well-being matters, and that they're seen as individuals. Getting employees to follow is a complex skillthat leaders must possess, so it's important to gain emotional support. Genuine emotional intelligence means that a leader appeals to employees' emotions, rather than just deliver commands.

3. **Set emotional intelligence goals.** A leader doesn't stop once he or she is able to get employees on board; he or she works to continually increase emotional intelligence in the team. This can be accomplished through things like constructive feedback and open communication. The next step is to set goals at different levels (for example, organization, team, and individual). There should be goals for each of the five pillars of emotional intelligence. Goals might resemble things like:

    - Ask a coworker for feedback on a task to show that you are approachable.
    - Eat lunch with a coworker you don't know very well.
    - Write down your emotional triggers and share them with the team.
    - Ask a coworker what motivates him or her, and genuinely listen to the answer.

Once the goals are set, coworkers should openly discuss them, even if it feels awkward. Following up is just as important as setting the goals, and with some practice, everyone will grow accustomed to the entire process.

The Importance of Emotional Intelligence in the Workplace

Of all the reasons that emotional intelligence is valuable in the workplace, there are two that are of paramount importance: job satisfaction andjob performance.

High emotional intelligence is correlated with increased job satisfaction. This includes employees whose coworkers and managers have high emotional intelligence. If an employee has high emotional intelligence (especially self- awareness), he or she has a low risk of burnout.

Overall, emotionally intelligent people tend to find more satisfaction and happiness in their jobs.

High emotional intelligence also fuels job performance. Employees who receive training in emotional intelligence are likely to be productive members of a team. In particular, those with great self-regulation skills tend to perform quite well at work. Emotional intelligence impacts job performance in seven ways:

1. ability to combine reason and emotion, empathize with other people, and express emotions
2. cognition
3. conscientious behavior
4. emotional stability
5. extroversion
6. self-efficacy
7. self-evaluations

Examples of Emotional Intelligence at Work

It's important to see what high (and low) emotional intelligence in the workplace looks like. Here are some examples.

1. Your office is making a change, and everyone will be using brand new software. If the workplace has an environment of high emotional intelligence, the change will likely be met by employees who take it seriously and are eager to learn. In contrast, a workplace with low emotional intelligence will will resist the change. Employees won't want to put in the effort to see it through. If the initiative itself isn't well-planned with consideration and thought, it's an indication that management lacks emotional intelligence and doesn't understand how big changes impact the employees.
2. A new work schedule has some employees upset. The abrupt change, made without their input, has affected many of their lives outside of work. An emotionally intelligent employee, who is adept at appropriately expressing his or her thoughts and emotions, will tactfully speak up and genuinely listen during the conversation. Conversely, an employee with low emotional intelligence might keep the emotions bottled up or complain to anyone nearby without any suggestions for a resolution.
3. An employee is having issues at home, and his overall mood is affected by the situation. A coworker or manager with high emotional intelligence will recognize that something's amiss, and compassionately offer a listening ear if he's so inclined. On the other hand, someone with low emotional intelligence will get annoyed at him, criticize him, or aggravate the situation.

4. Several employees in an office have young children, and therefore very busy home lives. An executive with high emotional intelligence will recognize and understand that his or her employees are people who have families. He or she will show flexibility, utilizing options such as the ability to work from home one day a week, knowing that it benefits everyone. In contrast, a supervisor with low emotional intelligence will not recognize (or care about) his or her employees' lives and responsibilities outside the workplace. Inflexibility is a sign of low emotional intelligence.
5. Meetings in your workplace don't always go smoothly. It becomes quite obvious which employees have high emotional intelligence, and which employees have low emotional intelligence. The former will attentively listen, keep everyone on task, and ensure that everyone has the opportunity to be heard. The latter, however, will offer no input, talk over his or her peers, zone out, or get into a heated argument.
6. Of course, it's not necessary to be best friends with your coworkers. A workplace that cultivated an environment of high emotional intelligence, though, is a place where employees enjoy spending time together. They might eat lunch together, go out together after work, or enjoy meeting up for social activities. Conversely, a workplace with low emotional intelligence is an environment where employees do not see value in building relationships.
7. Your restaurant has decided to completely redesign the menu, from entree choices to layout to graphics. If it's a workplace with high emotional intelligence, you might give the employees a chance to show their creativity and offer suggestions. It makes a team feel valued, upported, and heard; additionally, the employees can stretch their creative legs a bit. These employees feel invested in their work. Conversely, a workplace with low emotional intelligence always

strictly adheres to the same policiesit always has, even if the logic behind them is archaic and obsolete. Management in an emotionally unintelligent workplace is not concerned with employee input.

Chapter 6: Emotional Intelligence in a Relationship

A healthy relationship requires honesty, communication, and trust; we all know this. There's another element, though, that sometimes gets overshadowed. Emotional intelligence is important in a relationship because our ability to understand emotions helps us express them more effectively. Additionally, we recognize the impact that these emotions have on us and our partners.

You can tell if you and your partner have high emotional intelligence by examining your communication. Are you tapped into your partner's emotions? Are you able to handle difficult but necessary conversations? Of course, some people are prone to having emotionally intelligent characteristics, but the skills involved can be learned by anyone. Emotional intelligence has long-term benefits for you, your partner, and the well-being of your relationship. Emotional intelligence matters in a relationship for many valuable reasons.

First, emotional intelligence allows you and your partner to be wholly vulnerable with each other. Sometimes, vulnerability isn't easy, but it's necessary if you and your partner want to build a true connection. If you're holding back, but can identify and articulate why you're holding back, it's a sign of emotional intelligence. Understanding when to lower your guard, and how to go about doing it, also requires emotional intelligence. Moreover, if you're able to recognize a pattern of what makes you feel vulnerable, and you can communicate that with your partner, you're demonstrating emotional intelligence.

Emotional intelligence also means that you and your partner are good listeners. Understanding your own emotions, and understanding his or her needs, help make you a receptive listener. Listening is more important than you might think. Having a partner who actively listens decreases stress levels and improves emotional well-being.

A relationship with emotional intelligence means that the partners are able to empathize with one another. You not only recognize his or her needs, but also make them a priority. For someone who is emotionally intelligent, it's easy to pause your own issues and focus on what your partner is feeling. Your partner wants to feel seen and heard, and if you have high emotional intelligence, you understand his or her feelings. When both partners are empathetic, the bond strengthens.

Compromise is essential in any relationship. If you have high emotional intelligence, this skill is easy. Your empathy allows you to understand your partner's emotions and thoughts, even when they don't align with yours. It means that you're able to see your partner's perspective and thoughtfully come up with a resolution.

An emotionally intelligent person is an emotionally available person. This entails making your partner feel that he or she can open up to you. If your partner needs support or guidance, of course you want him or her to come to you. It's important to be in tune with your own emotions, and with those of your partner, so that you can ensure that he or she knows you're always there.

In an emotionally intelligent relationship, you're able to handle criticism and receive feedback well. This is important in the workplace, of course, but it's also essential in the context of a relationship. Being able to give or receive constructive criticism is a skill that prevents a communication shutdown. It's important to show one another that you're willing to learn, understand, and grow by accepting feedback and making necessary changes. It's crucial that you receive constructive criticism with openness, rather than react defensively or take it personally.

The ability to anticipate your partner's needs will help foster an emotionally intelligent environment for your relationship. It doesn't just mean knowing what he or she needs before you're even asked. It also includes things like understanding what he or she needs after a difficult day at work, supplying a shoulder to cry on, or remembering that he or she gets frightened by thunderstorms. It's also not about always saying exactly the right thing or finding exactly the right gift; rather, it's about showing your partner that you listen and care about his or her needs and wants. Emotional intelligence also makes it easier for you to ask what you need, and the response you receive is likely to be positive.

An emotionally intelligent person is able to clearly and respectfully express emotions. This includes standing up for himself or himself without having a discussion escalate into an argument. Verbalizing your needs is the only way you'll get them met. Articulating your needs means that you're genuinely sharing your feelings and asking for what you need from a partner.

Emotional intelligence helps us keep our focus on our priorities. It's important to know what you value in your relationship so that you can make a conscious effort to prioritize time for it.

In an emotionally intelligent relationship, two partners are able to swallow their pride, apologize to one another, and make up after a disagreement. It's not always the easiest thing to do, but it's a sign that you're preventing the buildup of resentment. Emotionally intelligent people aim to keep their connection strong, and they're more conscious of their accountability. They make amends because having a close bond with someone is much more important than being right. Emotional intelligence ensures that there aren't barriers between you and your partner. A disagreement should be productive; the goal is to come to a resolution together. Fights that escalate essentially poison a relationship. This skill needs and deserves nurturing.

In a relationship, it can be easy to take a partner for granted after a long time. If you have high emotional intelligence, though, you're able to recognize when you're not adequately appreciating your partner. This is the first step toward remedying the situation. Having emotional intelligence also means that you're able to recognize when your partner has unintentionally taken you for granted., rather than assume that certain behaviors are intentionally meant to upset you. It's essentially giving one another the benefit of the doubt without immediately jumping to conclusions, and always seeing the good in your partner.

It's essential in emotional intelligence that you're open to change. If you're in a long-term relationship, then chances are that you'll go through phases of change. We change careers, move to new homes, and adopt new habits. Revisiting or fighting change can put extra stress on a relationship. Emotionally intelligent people are able to understand change, and the need for it, while embracing new experiences.

Staying committed to your partner and your relationship is absolutely necessary for maintaining emotional intelligence. If you're in tune with your emotions and those of your partner, you realize how devastating it would be for either of you if infidelity broke your trust. Staying emotionally invested in your relationship includes always remaining conscientious of your partner's feelings.

Chapter 7: Emotional Intelligence for Leadership

To be an effective leader, you need to have a solid, fundamental understanding of your emotions and how your behavior impacts those around you. Relating to others and successfully cooperating are two necessary skills for leadership, and they both stem from emotional intelligence. Remember that there are five components of emotional intelligence: self-awareness, self- regulation, motivation, empathy, and social skills. We can take a look at each one and examine how they pertain to successful leadership.

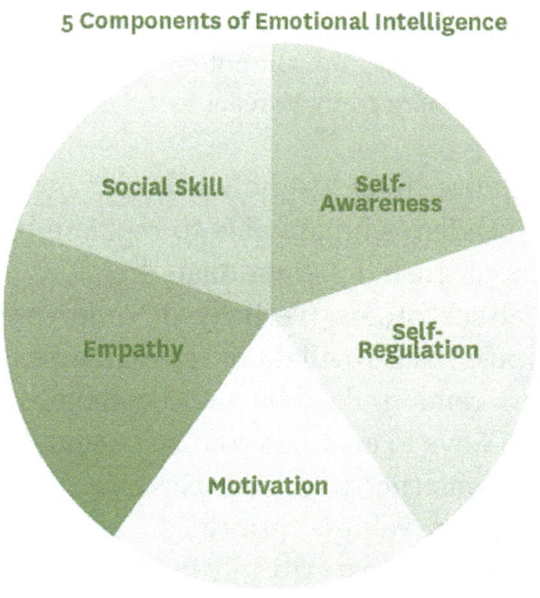

1. Self-awareness means that you're able to recognize how you're feeling, identify it, and articulate it. You also understand how your emotions and behaviors can influence others. In a position of leadership, this also includes having a clear and accurate perception of your weaknesses and strengths (and acting with humility). To improve your self-awareness, there are things you can do to practice. For instance, if you're feeling a strong emotion such as frustration or anger, stop. Take the time to explore why you're feeling what you're feeling. You can also write your thoughts in a personal journal; sometimes, writing down our thoughts reveals things about ourselves we didn't know. Above all, don't forget that your behaviors and reactions are your responsibility. You cannot control all situations, but you decide how you're going to react to it.

2. Self-regulation refers to how a leader is able to stay in control. Leaders who are able to regulate their emotions will seldom rush to emotional decisions, forfeit their values, attack others (verbally or otherwise), or assign stereotypes. Self-regulation encompasses a leader's ability to remain flexible and personally accountable. There are ways to enhance your self-regulatory skills. For example, construct your own personal al code of ethics. Include your values, priorities, and deal breakers. Knowing what's most critically important to you makes it quite easy to make a choice when you meet a moral decision. You can also practice holding yourself personally accountable. Some of us have the tendency to assign blame to others when things go awry, but an emotionally intelligent leader admits his or her mistakes and is ready for appropriate consequences. Stop blaming others, and you'll notice that you respect yourself more (others will respect you, too). To increase self-regulation, you can also practice calming yourself. Deep breathing might be a positive way to break the

habit of lashing out in a stressful situation. Additionally, just as with practicing self- awareness, journaling can be beneficial. Seeing your thoughts in writing makes it easier to evaluate them for fairness and accuracy. If you want, you can always tear up the paper when you've finished and throw it in the garbage.

3. Motivation for an effective leader comes from high expectations and the desire to achieve goals. This is known as intrinsic motivation, as actions are not fueled by wanting to impress others. Motivated leaders are typically optimistic; this mindset might not come naturally, but it's a valuable skill to master. A self-motivated leader always looks for the positive in a situation, even if it's a lesson learned from a failed attempt at something. There's always a positive takeaway; you just need to look for it. To help improve your self- motivation, there are things you can do to practice. For example, give some thought to why you enjoy your career. Why did you originally want this job? Are you struggling to remember? If you dig deeper and look at the root, you'll be able to view your situation from a different perspective. Since a self-motivated, emotionally intelligent leader designs goals and achievement plans, good practice can be re-evaluating your objectives and making sure you're staying on target.

4. Empathy is crucially important in leadership. If you want to successfully manage a team, you need to be able to put yourself in others' situations and see things from their perspectives. An empathetic leader gives constructive criticism, listens to team members when they need it, challenge employees who need to adjust behavior, and take the timeto help develop the individuals on his or her team. A

leader who shows empathy is able to earn a team's loyalty and respect. Improving your empathy is possible if you practice. For example, learn to understand body language. You can pay careful attention to your body language while you're listening to others speak to you. Body language can reveal a lot about how someone truly feels about a situation, and as an empathetic leader, you want your body language to convey openness, confidence, and trust. If you typically cross your arms or bite your lip while listening to someone, try eliminating those distracting cues. You should also learn to read other people's nonverbal cues so that you can assess how they feel and appropriately respond. Lastly, practice actively responding to others' feelings. If you can tell that someone is frustrated, let him or her know that you understand, and try to collaborate on a resolution for the situation.

5. Social skills are important for leaders, because a person with emotional intelligence is able to successfully communicate with others. It means that you're open to hearing others' thoughts, and you excel at rallying support for teamwork. Social skills are crucial for a leader; they're necessary for getting everyone excited about projects and ready for changes. A leader is also able to tactfully manage and resolve conflicts. A leader with social skills sets an example by working with his or her team, rather than delivering instructions and sitting back to watch others do the actual work. Building your social skills takes practice. For instance, you can educate yourself about conflict resolution. A leader must be skilled in this area, because tension can arise among coworkers, vendors, customers, or other collaborators. Conflict resolution is one of a leader's vital skills. You can also practice your communication skills by actively listening, thinking before you speak, and clarifying when necessary.

Lastly, you can enhance your team's loyalty by practicing praise. If someone has earned it, make the effort to praise him or her for a job well done. It can go a long way with employees.

Emotional intelligence might be a popular subject these

days, but scientifically speaking, it's a person's capability of perceiving and managing one's own (and other people's) emotions and comprehending emotional cues about relationships.

Rutgers psychologist Daniel Goleman diligently worked throughout the 1990s to research and explore emotional intelligence, a term that he had created. In 1998, in an article titled "What Makes a Leader," Goleman told the Harvard Business Review, "The most effective leaders are all alike in one crucial way: they all have a high degree of what has come to be known as emotional intelligence. It's not that IQ and technical skills are irrelevant. They do matter, but...they are the entry-level requirements for executive positions. My research, along with other recent studies, clearly shows that emotional intelligence is the *sine qua non* of leadership. Without it, a person can have the best training in the world, an incisive, analytical mind, and an endless supply of smart ideas, but he still won't make a great leader." Understanding the tenets of emotional intelligence as they apply to leadership is important because all five components are equally important. Deficiency in one of the areas can be the difference between a great leader and someone who could have been.

Daniel Goleman's Work

In 2001. Goleman collaborated with Annie McKee of University of Pennsylvania, and Case Western Reserve professor Richard Boyatzis. Together, the three explored in *Primal Leadership* the effects that emotions have in the workplace. The correlation between a company's financial success and the emotional state of its leaders, as it turned out, was undeniable. Seven years later, Goleman and Boyatzis published *Social Intelligence and the Biology of Leadership,* examining the natural structures that germinate emotional intelligence.

In 2008, Goleman's *The Focused Leader* showed us through research in neuroscience how successful leaders can improve each of the five tenets of emotional intelligence. He explained that focusing our attention, in large ways and small, can improve our emotional intelligence. Incidentally, it was 1990 when John Mayer and Peter Salovey coined the term "emotional intelligence." It was the same year of the invention of functional magnetic resonance imaging (fMRI). With fMRI, it was finally possible for neurologists to view the brain while active. Daniel Goleman focuses his research on the correlation between biological brain function as it pertains to emotional intelligence and the integral components of successful leadership. While some researchers have made counterarguments, Goleman maintains that it's not enough to just have technical skill and work ethic. An effective leader must also possess high emotional intelligence if he or she wishes to find success in the business world.

Chapter 8:

Are Women More Emotionally Intelligent Than Men?

When it comes to emotional intelligence, many people wonder if there are differences between men and women. Generally, females have more grey matter in the brain regions that process social information. This includes the interior frontal cortex (and the cortical folding therein), and the parietal cortex. Luckily, though, research shows that the three most gender-specific factors that influence a person's emotional intelligence are:

- emotional energy
- gender norms
- social role

Even if females are slightly more biologically prone to emotional intelligence, it's important to remember that all the skills involved can be learned by anyone. Even if you weren't born with a natural inclination toward high emotional intelligence, you can practice and master it. Moreover, a person's upbringing and culture play big roles in the development of emotional intelligence.

Empathy

Empathy refers to your ability to recognize emotional signals from others and to forge emotional bonds in various social situations. Having empathy means that you're able to identify and organize your emotions so that you can then verbally relay them.

In 2006, neuroscientist Tania Singer published the results of a study that evaluated neural responses to situations that can trigger empathy. The cerebral responses from women were substantially greater than those of men. A different study, led by researchers Simon Baron-Cohen, Barbara L. Ganzel in 2014, found that women's brains utilize the brain networks that are correlated to emotional and cognitive empathy.

Also in 2014, Neuroscience & Biobehavioral Reviews published a study about the empathetic differences between males and females. At all ages, on average, females had higher emotional intelligence than males; furthermore, a female's emotional quotient typically increases as she ages. Incidentally, children of both genders who have high emotional intelligence early in life continue to carry it throughout life.

Females' empathetic responses, from a neurological standpoint, tend to be more prevalent than those of males. Women also have a more robust connection between cognitive empathy and emotional empathy. The primary caretaker hypothesis, predicated on the idea that females are the ones who primarily take care of infants and will therefore develop and showcase skills associated with nurturing others, can explain the disparity. Prehistoric women were sole caretakers of the children, and they developed skills in recognizing emotions and empathetic response.

It's important to remember that a lot of the data that shows females having higher levels of empathy and emotional intelligence is self-reported. This can skew results if participants allow themselves to fall into the stereotypes associated with gender role norms. For example, a man might have the preconceived notion that men aren't "supposed to" be in tune with their emotions, and his answers might reflect that bias. Likewise, a woman might not want to supply a response that suggests she doesn't have high levels of empathy and emotional intelligence, because society has insisted for a long time that women must be nurturing, selfless, emotional caretakers.

It's important to remember that these, and any other research studies, do not account for every single man and woman. The results are generalizations based on data gleaned from a select group. You very well might not fall into either typicality.

Negotiations

We've all seen movies with aggressive, testosterone- fueled negotiations that seem to be an intense power struggle. In reality, though, successful negotiating requires finely tuned skills that are perhaps more subtle than the fist-pounding scenes we've seen in the media. Negotiations aren't designed to find a winner and a loser; rather, the goal is to collaborate to find resolutions. Historically speaking, business negotiations have been predominantly handled by men. It's women, though, whose innate emotional intelligence equips them to find success with this skill. Women are particularly good at negotiating for many reasons, such as: If you want to successfully negotiate, you must first build relationships. Mutual respect and understanding creates an environment where all parties will openly listen to other perspectives. It's important that participants are not concentrating on their own selfish needs. If there are relationships in place, people will see each other as human beings, not obstacles in the way of serving an agenda. A healthy relationship is a powerful way to bring together groups that disagree. In April of 2011, Dan Goleman asserted in Psychology Today, "Women tend to be better at emotional empathy than men, in general. This kind of empathy fosters rapport and chemistry. People who excel in emotional empathy make good counselors, teachers and group leaders because of this ability to sense in the moment how others are reacting." Negotiating requires a strong relationship and plenty of empathy; generally, women have an advantage in these departments.

1. To negotiate well, you must be able to accurately describe emotions, and express yourself both verbally and non-verbally. Women typically have an advantage here, because from the time they're little girls, society gives them permission to openly communicate their

feelings. Historically, females have been permitted to express their empathy more than males have. In contrast, men have generally been taught to keep their emotions hidden. Not having as much opportunity to be in touch with their own emotions can make it difficult to read other people's cues. In negotiations, it's essential to align emotional vibes to foster a level of comfort; however, it can be a challenge if you're not in tune with emotions. On emotional intelligence's importance in negotiating skills, Natalija Kaminskienė and Edward Kelly asserted in their 2016 study published in *International Comparative Jurisprudence*, "The effective negotiator or mediator must take into account not only the economic, political and physical aspects of the process, but also the emotional tenor of themselves as well as that of all of the parties." In very general terms, women have been given more opportunity to speak about feelings (their own and those of others), which is an advantage in the suitability of negotiating skills.

2. A negotiator's authority is not as important as his or her power of influence. Men generally enter negotiations with a sense of authority, possibly forgetting that most people are resistant to that. A negotiator's authority is not as important as his or her power of influence. Men generally enter negotiations with a sense of authority, possibly forgetting that most people are resistant to that.

Power can be intimidating to people, because there's always the underlying potential of abuse. Influence, in contrast, is more nuanced. Empathy for another person leads to a sense of trust that allows him or her to shift opinions toward where you'd like them to be. Building influence like this through empathy and relationships typically comes naturally to women. Generally, they have the ability to read a room and understand the consensus; it's a type of data collection that builds a woman's influence over a situation.

3. A negotiation is a compromise, and when you're navigating this, it's essential that you're sensitive to feedback. In 2016, the Harvard Business Review's study comparing male and female college students revealed that women were substantially more sensitive than males when it came to feedback from peers. It's important to have healthy self-esteem, of course, but it's just as important to value the feedback from others in negotiations. Listening, considering others' positions, and being open to others' perspectives are what keep a negotiation from just being an argument. Women are typically more sensitive to feedback than men.

"No doubt emotional intelligence is rarer than book smarts, but my experience says it is actually more important in the making of a leader. You just can't ignore it."

Jack Welch

Who are the Better Leaders?

Generally, women are natural leaders; however, that absolutely does not mean that men aren't as well. Today's workplace has become more well-rounded, and certainly virtual. Skills pertaining to emotional intelligence are now essential for success. If you're solely looking at empathy, then of course females tend to have an advantage. Emotional intelligence is more than just one of its integral tenets, though. A successful leader possesses a lot of different traits. For example, on average, men typically have higher levels of self-confidence than women. (Again, it's imperative to remember that generalizations will not apply to everyone.) The good news, for men and women alike, is that these skills can be practiced and improved.

Research studies show that there can be slight traditional gender differences among male and female workers, but disparities essentially dissipate among highly successful leaders. In executive positions of very large organizations, you'll find very confident women and very empathetic men.

While men and women have some biological differences that might give slight advantages in terms of building leadership skills, it's far more important to understand that one gender is not hardwired to be more successful than another. Emotional intelligence comprises various skills that are all very learnable. Never let gender role norms limit your ambition.

Chapter 9: Listening Skills

A large component of all five tenets of emotional intelligence is the ability to listen well. To be self-aware and to self-regulate, we must be able to listen to ourselves and others. Social skills, empathy, and motivation also require the ability to listen well. Listening is our way of receiving and interpreting messages from other sources, and it's essential in the process of communication. Without it, we can miss or misunderstand messages, and there's a breakdown of communication. Mastering listening skills is extremely valuable and absolutely worth your time and energy.

Many large organizations provide training for employees so they can build their listening skills. His makes sense if you consider the return on that investment: efficient work, fewer mistakes, customer satisfaction, and information sharing that can spark creativity and innovation. Leaders of industry will tell you that they wouldn't have found success without effective listening skills. The benefits include improved health, work performance, and confidence.

Hearing is Not Listening

The terms "hearing" and "listening" are often incorrectly used interchangeably. Hearing is an automatic process that your body performs. If you don't have a medical issue that impedes your ability to hear, it's simply a physical mechanism. Listening, in contrast, is an active and voluntary effort that requires concentration. Essentially, someone can hear what you're saying without actually listening.

Listening entails more than just the receipt of sound waves in your ears. It includes focusing your attention on the message, the speaker, his or her voice, and body language. Active listening means that you're engaged in the process with the speaker, aware of verbal and nonverbal messages, receiving and processing the information.

Time to Listen

We spend a lot of our time communicating with others, and a large portion of that is listening. A University of Missouri study found that 45% of our time communicating is spent listening.

Since we spend more time listening than any of the other activities, it makes sense that we should understand it better and practice the skills.

How We Communicate

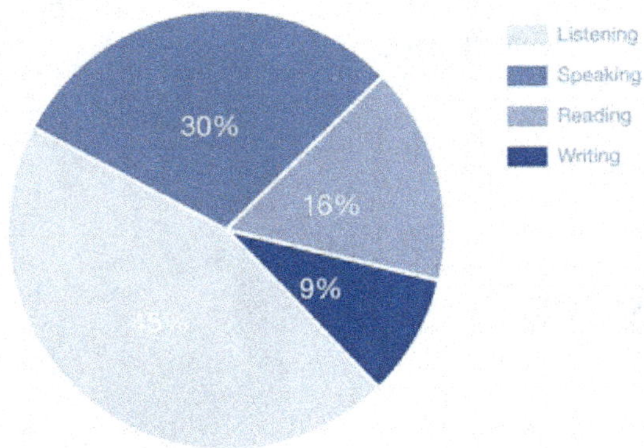

What is the Purpose of Listening?

We know that listening is an extremely important life skill, but what is the purpose of it?

Because listening serves numerous functions, its purpose can depend upon the situation and context of the communication. Some of the reasons we need listening skills are:

- to fully and accurately understand the speaker's ideas and perspective
- to show that we are interested and concerned
- to practice selflessness
- to detect nonverbal cues that accompany a speaker's words to increase our understanding
- to be able to critically think about the message being delivered
- to avoid distractions and focus on the message
- to come accept all views and come to an understanding
- to make the speaker feel comfortable enough to openly communicate

Thinking of ways to respond while someone is speaking is absolutely *not* a function of listening. It's important to focus on what is being said in order to gain understanding.

Obstacles to Listening Effectively

In the process of building effective listening skills, there can be barriers that get in the way. To improve your chances of success, it's a good idea to examine the common issues that can obstruct your path. What does it mean to be an ineffective listener?

It's quite typical to lose focus of what someone is saying and start thinking about what your response might be. Your mind might even drift to completely unrelated matters while the other person is talking. If you're thinking about anything other than what the speaker is communicating, it means that you're not fully listening. It's easy to think that you're getting the gist of it, but if you're not fully attentive, you'll miss what is being communicated.

We're all guilty of zoning out while someone has been speaking. Why do we do this? Part of the problem might be that, on average, a person speaks about 150 words per minute, and our brains process incoming information at approximately 600 words per minute. This disparity can cause your mind to wander. It can be difficult to focus on what a speaker is saying when your brain processes the words four times faster than they're being delivered.

There are other factors that can lead to our lack of focus. For example, if a speaker has an unfamiliar accent, speaks at an inappropriate speed or volume, or sounds inarticulate, clarity can be compromised.

We can also get distracted by other surrounding things. It's difficult to concentrate when there is outside noise, interesting things to view, or other distractions that pique our curiosity. Of course, this affects you if you're the listener; however, your lack of attention can be very obvious to those around you. Body language usually gives us away. The speaker could find this annoying, or even quite personally offensive. As a listener, it is your responsibility to filter the distractions.

Developing Your Skills

Technology has made it easy for us to easily communicate with one another, but we've also allowed it to erode our listening skills. Listening to someone shows a person that he or she is worth your time and energy. It's the glue that holds together problem solving, relationship building, and conflict resolution. Effective listening at work results in more accuracy and efficiency. It helps people build careers. Outside of work, effective listening can save a relationship. When raising children, teaching them good listening skills helps kids grow into resourceful, self-reliant adults.

We know that effective listening skills have numerous benefits. How can we improve our abilities? Here are ten things you can do to form good listening skills and habits.

1. Relax and focus. It's very important to show that you're attentive, but appearing rigid or nervous can make another person feel uncomfortable. Filter out surrounding activity and background noise. Don't allow your own feelings or thoughts distract you from listening to the speaker. Keep your attention on him or her.

2. Keep eye contact. It can be quite difficult to speak to someone who is looking at everything but you. At best, it can feel as though you have a portion of his or her attention. Eye contact is a very basic tenet of communication, and the only way you can accomplish

that is to look at a person when he or she is speaking to you. Put down your phone, leave the computer alone for the time being, and don't worry about papers on your desk. Even if he or she doesn't look at you (remember that some people can be shy or intimidated), continue to face the other person. It's not your place to correct his or her lack of eye contact; focus on yours. If a person is across the room, get up and move closer.

3. Silence the critic. Even if it's difficult, listen to someone without mentally passing judgment. There's no need to make criticisms in your head as that person speaks. He or she is conveying feelings and thoughts to you, and the only way you'll learn what they are is if you listen. Don't interrupt or attempt to finish someone's sentences just because he or she isn't getting to the point fast enough. The goal is to understand that person's thoughts and feelings, not to assign your own.

4. Visualize the speaker's words. In your mind, picture what this person is telling you. Is he or she telling you a story? Visualize the setting. Is the speaker discussing a concept? Have your brain organize the images. Remember key phrases by visualizing them spelled out. If you feel your mind starting to wander, snap back into focus. Above all, do not rehearse your response while someone is speaking.

5. Don't interrupt. If you watch television, you'll see people on reality and talk shows who aggressively yell to be heard. Interrupting or speaking over someone is obviously rude; however, it also sends messages to others.

These messages include:

- Your opinion does not matter to me.
- I don't care how you feel.
- What you think is not important.
- What I have to say right now is more important, relevant, accurate, or interesting.
- This is a competition, and winning means everything to me.

If your communication speed (thinking, processing, delivering) is faster than that of the speaker, it's your responsibility to align your tempo. Additionally, a speaker might not be looking for a solution, so don't jump to fix things. If a person wants your advice, he or she will request it. A lot of the time, a person is looking more for empathy and comfort, or just someone to listen while he or she works out a solution on his or her own.

6. Wait for a pause. We all have questions sometimes, and you might need to ask for clarity on something. Don't interrupt. Rather, wait for an appropriate pause and politely ask the speaker to revisit what was just said.

7. Keep your questions relevant. If someone is telling you a story, and a detail reminds you of something unrelated, do not take the conversation onto that tangent. It's inappropriate to shift the focus of what the speaker has been telling you. It can be difficult to work your way back to the initial matter. If you notice that you've asked something that has caused the speaker to drift away from the original topic, take accountability for it and redirect the conversation back to its original purpose.

8. Empathize. When someone is speaking, you should be able to sense how he or she is feeling. If the speaker is telling a story and expresses sadness, allow yourself to feel sad. Likewise, if he or she is expressing joy, allow yourself to feel that, too. Your facial expressions and other nonverbal communication will show the speaker that you're listening and invested. Good listening skills always require empathy. Sometimes, this requires concentration and effort, but it's worth it. There's no replacement for showing your empathy to someone who is speaking to you.

9. Provide feedback. If you're able to sense how the speaker feels, you should verbalize that by saying things like, "That must have been terrifying," "You and your family must be ecstatic," or "I'm so sorry that you've been enduring this awful ordeal." It really shows the speaker that you're listening. If his or her feelings are unclear, it's always okay to maintain eye contact, nod, and smile when he or she does. If the speaker is giving you instructions, always repeat them back to ensure that you've accurately understood the message.

10. Pay attention to nonverbal signals. We're able to glean a lot of information about one another without a single spoken word. Facial expressions and body language speak volumes, but you can also learn a lot over the telephone. A person's volume, cadence, tone, and pauses can give you insight to how he or she is feeling. If you're facing someone in person, your face will give you away if you're bored or annoyed. When you're listening, always remember that your nonverbal communication is just as important as the verbal.

Never Stop Practicing

Listening skills will grow rusty if you don't use them enough. Remember the ten tips for successfully listening to others and don't jump to conclusions. Ask for clarification if you're unsure if you're correctly understanding a message.

Chapter 10:

What are Emotions and Why Do We Have Them?

"Emotion" is a word that was first used in the early nineteenth century by Thomas Brown, and it became part of the modern English lexicon. Before that time, of course people had emotions; however, there wasn't yet a way for them to accurately communicate their understanding. Emotions may vary slightly among different cultures, but the basics are pretty universal. If someone doesn't have the ability to either perceive or express emotions, he or she is said to have alexithymia.

Defining emotion is incredibly difficult. Emotion is more than just a mental state, as it enmeshed with disposition, motivation, mood, personality, and temperament. Thoughts and feelings spark chemical and behavioral responses in our bodies. Emotions generate changes in our physiology, cognition, and behavior. In addition to psychology, the disciplines that are involved in contributing to research are:

- computer science
- endocrinology
- history
- medicine
- neuroscience
- sociology

Many theories have aimed to explain emotions' function, origin, and neurobiology; this typically has led to more research. Currently, PET scans and fMRI scans assist researchers study the brain's various processes. Cognition and emotion are undoubtedly intertwined, and the decisions we make rely on both.

Emotion can fuel motivation. Our feelings result in changes (both psychological and physical) that, in turn, impact our behavior. If you're a social, extroverted person, you likely openly express your emotions. In contrast, someone who is introverted is more likely to conceal them.

There are various components of emotions, such as:

- cognition
- expressive behavior
- psychological changes
- physiological changes
- instrumental behavior
- subjective behavior

These components complement each other as they comprise emotion. It's not enough to only look at one or two of the factors, but it's worth noting that different disciplines might use different language. For example, in psychology or philosophy, emotion is described in subjective terms that explore a person's conscious

experience; furthermore, it distinguished by physiological, biological, and psychological reactions.

Emotions can occur in the short term (anger, for example) or the long term (grief generally lasts awhile). Emotions exist in a continuum, and level of intensity can mean the difference between annoyance and rage. Emotions can fall into categories, but of course, there will be overlap. It can be more productive to examine the root and function of the emotion.

The Purpose of Emotion

Klaus Rainer Scherer, former director of the Swiss Center for Affective Sciences in Geneva, has devoted his work as a psychologist to studying emotion. He edited the Handbook of Affective Sciences, among other works, and developed an emotion model with five critical elements. It explores the coordination of systems during an emotional occurrence.

- Cognitive appraisal offers an analysis of surroundings and events.
- Physiological symptoms become present.
- Motor responses are prepared.
- Expression (vocal and facial) communicates the reaction.
- An emotion is subjectively identified once it has occurred.

It's important to remember that there is differentiation among similar words like "emotion," "mood," and "feeling." A *feeling* can represent emotion, but it doesn't necessarily include it. *Affect* describes how a person experiences an emotion or feeling. A *mood*, typically less intense but longer lasting than an emotion, is an affective state that doesn't always have a stimulus.

We respond to challenging things in lite, and sometimes, the response is our way of adapting. Emotions help this process. When we pay close attention to them, emotions can help provide effective solutions to problems.

Chapter 11: Transforming Emotions into Emotional Intelligence

For a long time, emotions have carried a stigma that suggests weakness. This is wholly untrue, though, and emotions are valuable. They're a natural part of us as humans, and they serve valuable purposes. How you handle them is what's important.

It is not realistic to expect a workplace to be void of emotions, but many of us are expected to put them aside when we're on the clock. It's normal for us to have emotional outbursts from time to time, but it's important to manage and regulate our own behavior. Anne Kreamer, who wrote *It's Always Personal*, asserts that it's neither healthy nor good for business to have a workplace that lacks emotion.

Women are especially susceptible to accusations that they're being "too emotional," since stereotypes have dictated that females' emotional intelligence makes them "unprofessional" or "weak."

Women and Emotion

We all know that emotion is a part of the human experience, but for a long time, it was viewed as something that was just for females. For many years, women have been described as emotionally unstable with unpredictable behavior such as outbursts of despair, jealousy, anger, and sadness; men have been portrayed as able to control themselves, especially in public. Women can still be tagged as "moody," "unreasonably emotional," or "irritable." This isn't just an unfair assessment; it can interfere with career advancement. There are still some people who believe that a woman's emotions should preclude her from positions of leadership. This gender stereotype is visible; if you look at top executive positions in many professions, women still hold fewer than half.

It can be true that women can overreact to issues or take comments and situations more personally than men, and it can also be true that men don't bring their feelings into the workplace as much as women do. Men and women have different wiring, and typically, a woman cries more often than a man does. (It's worth noting, according to Kreamer, that women generally have six times as much prolactin as men. Prolactin is the hormone in humans that controls tears.)

Historically, females have been raised to be nurturing caregivers, while men have been raised to be logical thinkers.

If women are biologically predisposed to cry more than men, raised to be emotional nurturers, likely to take words and situations more personally than men, underrepresented in positions of power, and labeled as emotionally unstable, does it mean they aren't cut out for success in leadership?

No. Of course not.

Women tend to be more emotional than men, but it only means that, in very general terms, males and females bring different things to the table. Anyone - male or female - who is blessed with the gift of emotion canand should convert it into emotional intelligence.

Emotions are Valuable

Abandon the idea that having emotions in the workplace is a disadvantage. "Emotions are signals thatsomething meaningful is happening," asserts author Dan Hill. "The trick is really to understand our emotions and to harness and manage them appropriately." Dan Hill wrote *Emotionomics: Leveraging Emotions for Business Success*. Eliminating emotion from the workplace would mean limiting freedom and creativity; instead, we should learn to understand the differences between fact and emotion. If we can do this in a professional manner, it will make us all stronger.

For people who are caring, compassionate, and gentle, chances are that you occasionally shed tears. This can be problematic in the workplace, only because others can label it as a weakness and use it in a manipulative way. If you feel your emotions start to get away from you, take a step away. It's always best to take a few moments to decompress and gather your thoughts.

For long-term success, it's in no one's best interest to encourage a robotic culture at work. Humans are individuals, and we all have emotions. Translating emotions into good feelings is conducive to productivity and efficiency in an organization. Emotional intelligence leads to career growth and professional success, and emotions should be viewed as an advantage. Applying them appropriately is the key.

Emotions can be perceived as negative if they are not appropriately managed. It can become a balancing act between not wanting to be perceived as cold and heartless, and sharing too much at work. Remember that emotions are part of what it means to be human and being in touch with yours is a positive quality.

Convert Emotions into Emotional Intelligence

Well-managed emotions are beneficial in a workplace. Translating them into emotional intelligence is valuable for an organization's success. For example, sensitivity to emotions can mean that you're able to recognize displeasure in a coworker or client, and therefore quickly remedy the situation before it escalates. Building networked and developing relationships also require a skill set that includes social skills, self-awareness, motivation, self-regulation, and empathy. Relationships are essential to success.

If you're a caring, sensitive person, you might have had people tell you that those are weaknesses. That's entirely untrue; furthermore, you have an advantage when it comes to winning people over. It's time to abandon the notion that emotions are illogical and distracting liabilities that don't belong in the workplace. It's necessary to truly understand emotions and embrace them.

If you feel that your emotions get in the way when you're trying to work, you can regain control and utilize a combination of logical cognition and emotion. Remember that all decisions are influenced by feelings. This is an advantage when you're proud of your work, confident in your success, and passionate in your effort.

Chapter 12: Manage Your Negative Emotions

Many of us don't like feeling angry, frightened, or sad; we tend to have an adverse response to emotions that we feel are negative. Many of us would prefer to stay optimistic and positive, feeling cheerful and joyful. In fact, many of us were probably raised to always look at the bright side, not get angry, and keep our chins up when we felt sad. Maybe you've even felt severely anxious and did your best to just calm down.

None of these things is bad, and of course you don't want to feel negative emotions. It's important to realize, though, that emotions are neither good nor bad; they just *are*. Some might feel negative, but they're really just part of the human experience. Moreover, sometimes an emotion (for example, anxiety) is merely symptomatic of a larger issue. Your brain could be trying to get you to recognize what's going on. Think of it as a fever indicating that you have an infection somewhere in your body. Anxiety can mean that you need to invest in some self-care.

Not wanting to deal with difficult emotions means that we have very unrealistic expectations of life. Rather than viewing them as negative, we can look at them as valuable. Our emotions can be telling and powerful; we need to understand and embrace them. Life is sometimes challenging, but we shouldn't shy away from emotions just because they make us uncomfortable.

Negative Emotions

How can we embrace "negative" emotions and live a fulfilling life? Whether or not you want to admit it, emotions that make you feel bad or uncomfortable are there. Most people don't love feeling anger, despair, disappointment, disgust, frustration, guilt, sadness, and shame, but we all feel these things.

Paul Eckman, a psychologist who pioneered the study of emotions, asserted in the 1970s that there are six fundamental emotions:

- anger
- disgust
- fear
- happiness
- sadness
- surprise

You might notice that four of these are perceived as"negative" emotions.

Ten years later, psychologist Robert Plutchik elaborated on Eckman's fundamentals. Plutchik stayed that there were actually eight emotions:

- anger
- anticipation
- disgust
- fear

- joy
- sadness
- surprise
- Trust
-

Both Eckman and Plutchik elaborated on their findings and included a range of emotions with varying intensities. The wheel of emotions showcases this spectrum.

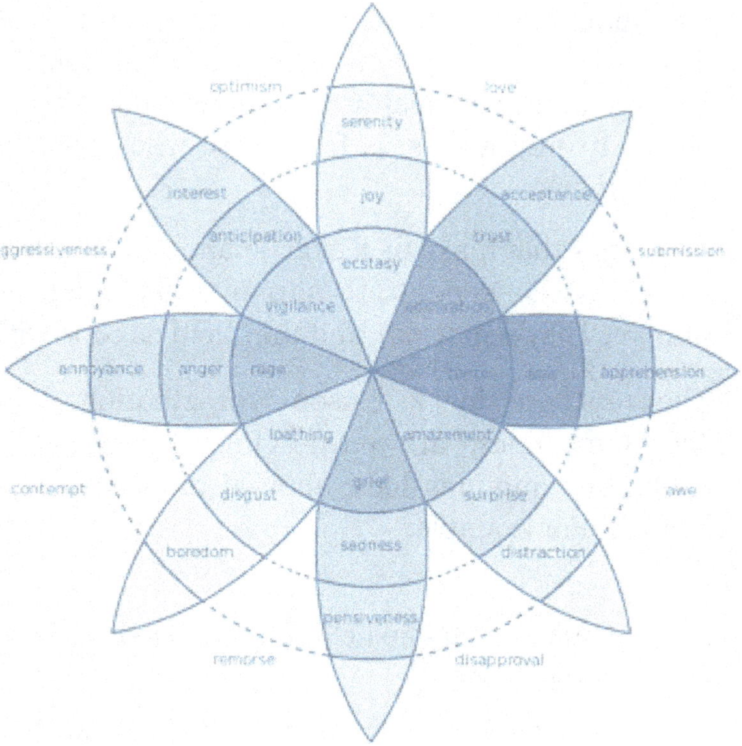

Negative Emotions Aren't Actually Negative

It might be hard to believe, but the emotions that we perceive as negative can actually be good for us for many reasons.

1. They're completely normal. At some point in our lives, we started to believe that "negative" emotions were bad. Of course, it's important to be

   present and live a life with gratitude but expecting joy 100% of the time is incredibly unrealistic. What's more, we should feel open to discussing the "negative" emotions, because they're completely natural. Everyone has them. If we qualify the undesirable emotions as "bad," it only makes us feel worse when we feel them. Emotions

   - the ones that make us feel good and the ones that make us feel not-so-good - are part of what it means to be human. They're normal, and they help us cope with life.

2. They're there for a reason. All emotions, even the "negative" ones, are purposeful. Throughout human evolution, emotions have allowed us to survive and be healthy. For example:

3.

   - Guilt and shame help us adhere to our own moral codes.
   - Anger protects us by motivating change.
   - Fear signals danger
   - Sadness builds empathy and connectivity

We've needed all these emotions to survive the evolutionary process. They might not be fun to experience, but they're there for a reason. It's up to us to determine their purpose in our lives. "Negative" emotions urge us to progress and mature.

4. They alert us. Emotions can act as signals that something is amiss. If you're feeling off-track or disjointed, emotions can catch your attention to alert you. Chances are, you'll experience moderate emotions at first. Annoyance, irritability, and frustration can be your brain's way of trying to gently tell you that something isn't right. If you ignore those, the alerts become more obvious, and you'll experience stronger emotions like anger or fear. Unfortunately, some of us can ignore these signals, too, and our brains are essentially forced to get more aggressive with the messages. Emotions start to snowball into things like depression and rage. It's so important to listen to our bodies and our minds.

5. They motivate us. Emotions can serve as catalysts for change. In some scenarios, we might not have taken action if it hadn't been for our feelings of anger. It can prompt you to take charge and speak up. Recognizing, embracing, and channeling our anger can be extremely powerful. Dr. Martin Luther King, Jr., told us, "The supreme task is to organize and unite people so that their anger becomes a transforming force." When you feel "negative" emotions, they can be the push that you need to be productive and solve problems.

6. They allow us to let go. It's no secret that ignoring our emotions can lead to serious health issues. If we give ourselves permission to feel our emotions, especially the

difficult ones, it means we can also let it go and move on with our lives. If we don't deal with the emotions, they'll fester; if we embrace the emotions, we can then release them. The goal is not to have these emotions stew inside you forever, and it's also not to embrace them to the point of drowning in them. Some emotions are unpleasant, difficult, and painful, but embracing them is the only way you'll ever be able to let them go. A good cry is an appropriate analogy here. If you allow yourself to break down and have a cathartic cry, you'll feel lighter and less burdened once you've finished.

7. You'll live a fulfilling life. We've seen in various cultures and philosophies that light and dark complement one another.

Perhaps you've read motivational quotes about only being able to appreciate sunny days by experiencing the rainy ones. As cliché as that might be, the sentiment is spot-on. Seeking equilibrium, understanding interconnectivity, and appreciating complementary forces will help you live a life of balance. The opposite forces of emotions allow us to be fulfilled. It's important to truly feel a wide range of emotions.

8. They make us stronger. Think of “negative” emotions as germs. Once you’ve fought off a virus, your immune system strengthens, and you’re more resilient the next time you get a cold. The more you deal with “negative” emotions, the tougher you become. The next time that emotion comes along, you’re equipped to handle it. You know how to best cope with it, and you recognize that it’s temporary. By dealing with your emotions, you’re building your coping skills as a sort of immune system. The more you practice your coping skills, the stronger and more effective they become. You don’t want to hide from your emotions; be ready to handle them when they come.

Turning the Negative into Positive

Remember, we don’t want to erase “negative” emotions. It’s beneficial, though, to make the experience positive by understanding the value and purpose. The RISE process can help you remember how to learn from emotions that are uncomfortable.

R - Recognize the emotion. Allow yourself to feel it. Don’t just push it away. Don’t let it take over, but be present in the emotion. Acknowledge it, then release it.

I - Identify your emotion’s purpose. Is it an alert? Is it your brain’s way of offering you protection? Is it designed to motivate you effect some change? Consider why you’re experiencing this emotion.

S - Stop and check. Most of the time, our "negative" emotions are justified, but sometimes, they're misguided. Pause to consider if you have all the facts before embracing your anger at a family member. If you're feeling anxious, is it because there are things to legitimately worry about, or have you created a bad habit of worrying too much? If you're feeling disappointed by someone's actions, think about the role you play in the situation.

E - Establish a plan. It's time to figure out your action. It could be something like showing gratitude for the gift of fear and its purpose to keep you out of danger, or it could be something like channeling your frustration at work into speaking up for yourself. It's also perfectly okay to have your plan be to just feel the emotion.

As discussed in Chapter 11, emotions are neither positive nor negative. Having said that, though, we know that many of us have difficulty handling emotions that cause us stress.

Managing difficult emotions can be a real challenge. They're inevitable, of course, and we all experience them at one time or another. When we attempt to avoid them, though - by ignoring them, diverting our attention, or stifling them - we actually get the opposite of the desired effect. This exacerbates the situation, and those emotions tend to magnify. It sounds counterintuitive but trying to avoid difficult emotions results in having to experience them even more intensely.

We need to be careful not to have a perfectionist mindset when it comes to our emotions. It's unrealistic to expect that our emotions will always be positive, but it can also be very problematic. Self-compassion and patience are necessary if we're to accept that difficult emotions are completely normal and unavoidable. A healthy perspective includes remembering that we should always seek balance.

You'll recall from Chapter 11 that your emotions are essentially messages from yourself to yourself. They're symptoms that supply clues to larger issues. It's important not to ignore the messages, because they provide us with valuable data. That relevant information can be used to help identify a larger issue, shift your priorities, make decisions, and solve problems. Don't forget, though, your RISE process - particularly, the third step when you stop to determine if you have all the necessary and accurate information. If you do, then it benefits you to incorporate that into your choices. Highly successful and emotionally intelligent people don't try to erase emotion from their decision making; rather, they put emotions' value to work for them.

Managing your emotions, especially the difficult or challenging ones, is beneficial for your ability to perform your best. It also improves your general well-being and peace of mind. We can show ourselves compassion and patience, knowing that it's perfectly natural to experience difficult emotions. A practical and very valuable application is meditation. It's an effective way to handle stress and anxiety so that you can face the challenging emotions with a clear head.

Self-Compassion

Self-care, both emotionally and mentally, begins with compassion for yourself. Most of us have inner critics that can be quite severe; we'd likely never speak to a close friend the way we speak to ourselves. During a challenging time, it's especially important to treat yourself with kindness and patience. Research shows that people who show themselves compassion are typically less lazy and weak. Additionally, they're more self-aware, honest with themselves, and well-equipped to effectively navigate transitions and stumbling blocks.

To incorporate self-compassion in your life, there are strategies you can utilize. Think about how you speak to yourself. Does the inner voice tell you that you're not good enough? A lot of us speak to ourselves this way, even though we'd never think to be so harsh to our loved ones. Start taking note of the language you use when you speak negatively to yourself. Are you berating yourself for going through a tough time?

Emotional Intelligence

The best way to manage your own challenging emotions and understand the emotions of others is to build your emotional intelligence. You'll recall that there are five basic tenets of emotional intelligence and incorporating four of these elements can help you handle emotions that are uncomfortable or difficult. It begins with self- awareness; you must first know and understand your own emotions. You need to be able to recognize and accurately identify what it is you're feeling. Self-regulation means that you're using your skills and resources to manage your emotions so that you don't impulsively react without thinking. Empathy and compassion are required, and you must show yourself the kindness you would extend to a loved one in the same situation. Lastly, motivation is the inner drive you need to want to grow as a person. Without it, you'd lose sight of why you're even working on managing the emotions.

Chapter 13: Resilience

Mental and emotional resilience refers to your ability to cope during a critical situation and quickly return to a normal state. Resilience is the result of developing strategies to stay calm during chaos and move on.

We all face stressors every day, and some of us are able to withstand more than others. Persistent stress wreaks havoc on your sense of balance if you haven't built resilience. It encompasses mental, physical, and emotional adaptations and coping skills. If you're resilient, it means you're able to bounce back from adversity, stronger than before.

In 1973, the first resilience research was published. It explored, through epidemiology, the coping mechanisms that we now know are part of resilience. Researchers also developed instruments to examine systems that support resilience development.

Researchers have done extensive work exploring the underlying issues that result in the need for resilience. For example, poverty, mistreatment or abuse, and disastrous events can affect a person in ways that warrant coping mechanisms. There are some factors, such as family bonds, mentors, and school influence, that can contribute to ensuring that those coping mechanisms provide positive outcomes.

Resilience is a process, not a character trait. Research has found that resilience is the positive outcome when a person has the ability to interact with elements that will protect them from danger and promote General well- being. When a person encounters a detrimental situation, he or she can approach it in one of three ways:

- angry or volatile outburst
- numbness and inability to react
- upset over the change

Resilient people react in the third fashion. They become upset, make necessary changes, and cope. The other two choices tend to result in assuming the role of a victim; placing blame or avoiding coping strategies typically do not foster growth or promote well-being. The goal is to respond to a circumstance, rather than have an impulse reaction. This can be tricky, since "negative" emotions such as fear and anxiety tend to impede our ability to tackle issues.

Thoughtfully responding means that you can put an end to whatever the crisis is, cope, and bounce back.

Positive Factors

Coping strategies tend to be successful when coupled with positive factors that facilitate resilience. For example, you might be in an emotionally safe space to cope because you have positive surroundings like family, community, or school.

Biological Connections

Three foundations of resilience - self-concept, self- esteem, and self-confidence - spawn from three specific nervous systems (central nervous system, autonomic nervous system, and somatic nervous system, respectively).

Resilience can be especially important if you experience multiple crises. It takes a toll on the human body; chronic anxiety and constant worrying will diminish your body's immune system, making your susceptible to illness.

Resilience to stress has a neurobiological foundation. Your brain responds to elevated cortisol levels (brought on by stress) and decreases sympathetic nervous system activity. Resilience, which is a positive adaptation, plays a role in your long-term health and well-being.

Bouncing Back

We all face hardships and adversities in life. Resilience means that you don't allow those circumstances to define you or defeat you. Setbacks and failures can knock you down, but it's important to come back just as strong. Resilience is a part of emotional intelligence; some of the factors include:

- emotional regulation
- optimism
- positive attitude
- viewing setbacks as opportunities

If you're resilient, it means that you learn from mistakes and failures, and you value those lessons. Remaining optimistic helps your mind and body cope with a disturbing experience. This means that you're able to access all of your valuable cognitive resources, making it much easier to calmly analyze what has happened and consider a path for moving forward. Remember, resilience is not a character trait; it's an active process that requires determination and dedication. The payoff, though, is achieving goals even after unfortunate things have happened.

The goal is not to avoid or reject pain and disappointment; rather, resilience allows us to get through it without having it take over. It can be difficult to persist after trauma or misfortune. Are you resilient? There are some questions you should ask yourself. Do you solely blame yourself and your inadequacies for setbacks in your life? Do you demand and expect perfection from yourself at all times? A resilient person realizes that sometimes there are contributing factors, and life has ups and downs.

Setbacks Make Us Stronger

Crises can be overcome, and we can come out stronger on the other side. Failure - as much as list of us dislike that word - is natural. It's a part of every human's life. It's important to remember, though, that introspection, learning, and transcendence are also natural. Failure isn't a brick wall; it's a stumbling block. Learning lessons from our failures is how we grow to be humble, mature, and empathetic. You might have the urge to harshly judge yourself, but resist it. You're developing your self- regulation, and your emotional intelligence will improve because of it.

Chapter 14: Bouncing Back from Adversity to Succeed

As discussed in Chapter 13, resilience is a key component to success and overall well-being. Adversity is a part of everyone's life, at one point or another. How do you respond when it happens? It's your resilience that allows you to bounce back after a failure or disappointment, and it's this ability that will always play a large role in your ability to live a fulfilling and successful life.

When problems arise, as they do, sometimes it can be difficult to resist the urge to pull the covers over your head. It can make a person feel helpless and unable to move forward. Resilience is what will get you to embrace the setbacks with confidence and determine how to cope.

It's important to not let pitfalls get in the way of success. In order to bounce back from adversity, you need bravery, determination, and effective strategies. Here are 13 ways that you can develop resilience.

1. Convert the difficulty into a personal challenge. Even a small thing like adjusting your vocabulary can facilitate your resilience development. Instead of perceiving a hardship as a failure or even a difficulty, think of it as a challenge or an opportunity. Shifting your mindset can be energizing, and you're more likely to face a challenge with determination. If you look at a tough situation as a disaster, you're likely to view yourself as a suffering victim. Turn your negative predicament into a positive opportunity to make changes. In order to be productive, you want your body and mind to feel relaxed and focused, and if you tell yourself that you're facing a challenge, your body will release cell-repairing hormones that encourage the efficient use of bodily energy. The alternative is to view your circumstances as perilous, and your body will respond with increased anxiety, blood pressure, and blood glucose levels. Adjusting your wording is more than

just a matter of semantics here; it will benefit your mental and physical health.

2. Visualize success. Think about how you want your life to look. As clearly as you possibly can, visualize it. How can you make that happen? Once you can see what the goal looks like, you can construct a plan with steps to follow in order to reach it. When you face adversity, this is especially important. How do you want your life to look once you come out on the other side? Give this question some serious thought and allow yourself to answer it with as much detail as you can.

3. Seek out a role model. Is there someone whom you admire that has dealt with adversity before? Examine a resilient person's way of dealing with hardship and model your own rules to align with what you find. You can become more resilient if you find someone you can study. It can be someone living or dead, famous or not. A great example of a model is Helen Keller, who lost both her sight and hearing early in childhood. She overcame seemingly insurmountable obstacles just to learn to accurately and effectively communicate, and she went on to graduate from college, write numerous books, and helped found the American Civil Liberties Union. It probably would have been easy for Ms. Keller to throw in the towel early on in life, allowing others to do everything for her. She embodied resilience, though, and she continues to serve as an excellent role model. If you're feeling discouraged or defeated, you can ask yourself, "What would Helen Keller do?" Choose someone who will inspire you to always get back up and gather your strength.

4. Meditate. Practicing mindfulness can help replenish your clarity, strength, and perspective. Meditation teaches us to skip the judgment and simply acknowledge our own thoughts. Finding an inner balance that embodies self-awareness and self-care protects us from external stressors. Building and developing this balance makes us more resilient.

5. Find the meaning. When you face adversity, it's best to draw meaning from the experience. If something unexpected happens, look for ways to find positive meaning. What can you gain from these circumstances? A negative situation is not merely a waste of your time and energy. Look at what has happened and ask yourself what you can learn from it. Is it an opportunity to master new skills that will likely be useful again in the future? Is this situation making you a more well-rounded person? Is it a good chance to practice patience? You can always derive something positive from even truly terrible circumstances, and you owe it to yourself to find the meaning.

6. Practice flexibility. Having the ability to adjust when you need to comes from mental flexibility. It's important to be able to shift gears if circumstances require it, and sometimes a situation offers several options. Flexibility allows you to weigh options and effectively respond. Conditions can vary, and the ability to adjust makes it much easier to solve problems. The alternative it to struggle the entire way, essentially swimming against the current. You can practice these skills when stakes aren't as high in order to develop mental flexibility. Adjusting your strategy in response to circumstances, events, or others' actions helps build your flexibility, and therefore your resilience.

7. Get active. Your thinking should be proactive rather than reactive. That is to say, action comes from active thinking. Getting yourself to the other side of a negative situation requires action, and therefore active thinking. Try asking yourself questions, such as:
   - What can I do to restrict this issue so that it doesn't escalate?
   - What can I do to decrease the potential drawbacks of this issue?
   - How can I most effectively respond to this?
   - Which factors can I control?
   - How can I maximize the potential benefits of this issue?
   - How can I solve this issue in the most efficient way possible?

8. Make connections. Relationships with others can provide a strong support system, and it's important to be able to rely on trusted family and friends with things go awry. Getting yourself to the other side of adversity is easier if you surround yourself with people who have your best interest in mind. Attempting to navigate a crisis and its fallout can be extremely difficult if you do it alone, and there are people who are willing to listen and help you.

9. Practice self-care. Nurturing yourself facilitates adjusting your outlook. In order to convert anxiety to positive, productive energy, you need to take care of yourself. This can mean reading or watching inspirational stories, spending time in nature, listening to music, talking with close friends, exercising, and a ton of other things. If you expect your mind and body to be able to perform for you, you need to nurture yourself.

10. Inventory your strengths. Surely, you've faced adversity in the past. Which personal strengths were you able to tap into in order to successfully get past it? Are they strengths that you can apply to your current circumstances? Maybe you have remarkable patience, great mediating skills, or a strong religious faith that helped see you through a tough time. Maybe you have a fantastic sense of humor that allowed you to more easily cope with hardship. Whatever those strengths were, they're in your reserve. Pull them out and put them to work for you.

11. Don't get yourself stuck. We can all get ourselves trapped in a vicious cycle of overthinking and essentially making problems worse. It can quickly spiral out of control. It is not productive to continually so yourself how something like this possibly could have happened to you. It's also a waste of time and energy to think about whom you can blame for certain circumstances. We can all get ourselves into these mind traps, but they'll work against you rather than for you. Thinking this way will bring you to a dead end. It's much more positive and productive to think about ways to solve a problem or get yourself through a difficult situation that you're facing.

12. Be realistic. Of course, resilience requires confidence and optimism, but it's important not to confuse those things with delusion that everything is fine and will work itself out on its own. A resilient person is optimistic, but realistically so; it means seeing a situation at face value and having the confidence to take appropriate action. Overcoming adversity is an active process; it does not mean merely pretending that a hardship is not real. Resilience requires the confidence that you're capable of overcoming the obstacle and continuing forward with your life.

13. Leave your comfort zone. Stress can wreak havoc on your mind and body. It's extremely important to build a resistance to it in the same way that you activate your immune system by receiving a vaccination for a virus. Being introduced to a small amount of a disease forces your body to learn to cope with it. Psychological resilience works the same way, in that exposure to stressful circumstances force you out of your comfort zone. This can mean things like climbing a mountain to conquer a fear of heights, going out by yourself to network and meet new people, or learning a new language. You can gradually increase the challenges you give yourself. Your resilience will become enhanced by the way you build immunity to stress. When an adverse situation arises, you'll be better equipped to manage it.

Achieve Your Goals

At one point or another, everyone deals with disappointment, failure, and adversity. It's part of the human experience. It's important to be able to bounce back from these circumstances, because otherwise, we'd just be stuck. In order to achieve goals and realize success, we must be able to work our way through the difficulties.

Chapter 15:
The Motivation to Change

What is Motivation?

As previously mentioned, motivation is one of the five basic tenets of emotional intelligence. In practical terms, we can look at what it encompasses. Motivation is:

- taking initiative and persisting toward a goal
- determination
- resisting old, unhealthy patterns and habits
- a drive (internal or external) that makes you take action
- devoting your time, focus, and energy to the pursuit of a goal
- the pursuit of change despite stress, fatigue, or boredom
- doing everything you can to effect change

K. Anders Ericsson

Dr. K. Anders Ericsson, a psychologist and professor at Florida State University, has completed extensive research on the psychological aspects of success, expertise, and performance.

Dr. Ericsson asserts that, of all the predictors of success, a person's motivation has the most substantial impact. Perhaps you've heard the phrase that Dr. Ericsson once coined, "It takes ten years and 10,000 years to become an expert." His research supports that this is true in all aspects, including athletics, academics, and business. Success comes from persisting over time without giving up. The robust correlation between success and motivation shows that if you're highly motivated, you will thoroughly prepare. If you thoroughly prepare, you will achieve positive results.

Motivation's Impact

If you're making changes in your life, you know that it can be quite difficult. Habits are challenging to replace, especially if you've had them for a long time. Motivation is necessary for making lifestyle changes. Your ability to end the cycle of long-term patterns and habits relies heavily on the motivation you have for making positive and lasting changes.

Talk is cheap, and merely saying that you're motivated to make changes doesn't mean that you have the drive to achieve the goals you've set for yourself. Being truly motivated is essential because it affects your efforts in many different ways.

To achieve the changes that you desire, you'll need to:

- prepare yourself to make adjustments
- remember patience because change takes time
- persist even when your old habits are stubborn
- persevere to tackle obstacles
- implement supports

Internal vs. External

Everyone experiences different motivations that drive him or her to change. Motivation can be positive or negative, and it can also be internal or external. The following chart categorizes different types of motivation, so that you can see the various outcomes.

Types of Motivation

	Positive	**Negative**
Internal	Self-validation Satisfaction Challenge Desire Passion	Insecurity Threat Fear of failure Feelings of inadequacy
	Typical outcome: fulfillment, success	Typical outcome: a little change,but Chance of relapse

External	Recognition from others Financial gain Typical outcome: positive feelings, continued dependency on others for validation, some change	Lack of respect from other people Fear of loss (job, relationship, etc.) Instability Financial or social stress Pressure from partner Typical outcome: a little change, large chance of relapse

Clearly, it's ideal to have motivation that is both internal and positive, because it stems from confidence, safety, and strength. The other three combinations of motivation can yield positive results, of course, but the success rate is far less than if your driving forces are positive and come from within. If you find that your motivating factors come from the other three quadrants, it's a good idea to reassess your motivations so that you can make a shift in what fuels you to take action.

Putting in the Effort

Once you have goals set and you're ready to take action toward making changes in your life, remember that you will get out of it what you put into it. In other words, if you've identified goals and constructed a plan, but don't take any steps to make changes, you will see zero results. Likewise, if you devote time, focus, and energy to making changes, you will see results. A lot of people will tell you that they want to change, but they don't mention anything about wanting to do the necessary work. When there is a disparity between the goals that you've set for yourself and the amount of effort your exerting, you need to make an adjustment. The gap between goals and effort needs to be filled so that they are in alignment. Will you do that by changing your goals to match the effort, or vice versus?

Making serious changes is easier said than done, but if you are genuinely motivated, expect to put in the necessary work so that you can reach your goals.

Tough Times

We know that making life changes can be difficult, and the work involved in achieving success can sometimes get tedious or challenging. It can get stressful and exhausting at times, and it's during those times that maintaining your motivation is the most important. Your path to success will likely begin with a lot of inspiration and energy, but that typically wanes over time. The rough times are the true test of your motivation; how you handle yourself during these times will determine whether or not you're able to make changes and maintain them. Some people will give up when it gets difficult, but if you are truly motivated, you will keep pushing forward. You'll keep going because you know the work is worth the reward.

Most people don't love these tough times, but some actually enjoy the extra challenge. It's much more about how you respond to the circumstances, and that generally varies from person to person. You don't have to love when it turns into a grind, but it's important to accept that your journey has parts that can be difficult. It might not feel great at the time, but the success will be worth it.

Find Motivation with the Three Ps

When you have a goal to make changes in your life, finding motivation means staying consistent and not giving up when it seems like an easy way out. Motivation to change starts with the three Ps: path, preference, and promise.

Path refers to which direction you're going. Of course, one path is the one you've been on for awhile, and it's an option to just stay on it. You could also choose a path that makes more gradual changes over time, or a path that incorporates instant, drastic changes.

Preference refers to which of the three paths you've chosen. One isn't better than another; they're all options. It's up to you to choose which works best for you in the circumstances you're in at the time. Your preference will reflect whether or not you're going to make changes, how much effort you'll need to invest, and what your goals are.

Promise refers to the agreement you'll make with yourself. You'll need to dedicate time and energy to your path toward success, and you should make a promise to yourself that you'll do the work to make the changes. Your decision to make changes was just the beginning; now, you need to remain dedicated and motivated to see it through.

Practical Tips for Finding Motivation

It certainly can be difficult to find and maintain motivation to change. Without change, though, we don't grow. As George Bernard Shaw once said, "Progress is impossible without change, and those who cannot change their minds cannot change anything." Here are three pieces of advice that can help you find the motivation you need.

1. Find a role model whose positive habits you admire and can emulate. His or her story of success can inspire you to stay motivated.

2. Remain patient and dedicated. Visualize how your life will look once you've reached your goals and remember that getting there will require patiently adhering to your plan.

3. Do it for yourself. If you're working to improve your life, remember that your motivation should be positive and internal. You're taking care of yourself, not making changes to try to please others.

Chapter 16: Emotional Response Versus Logic and Decision Making

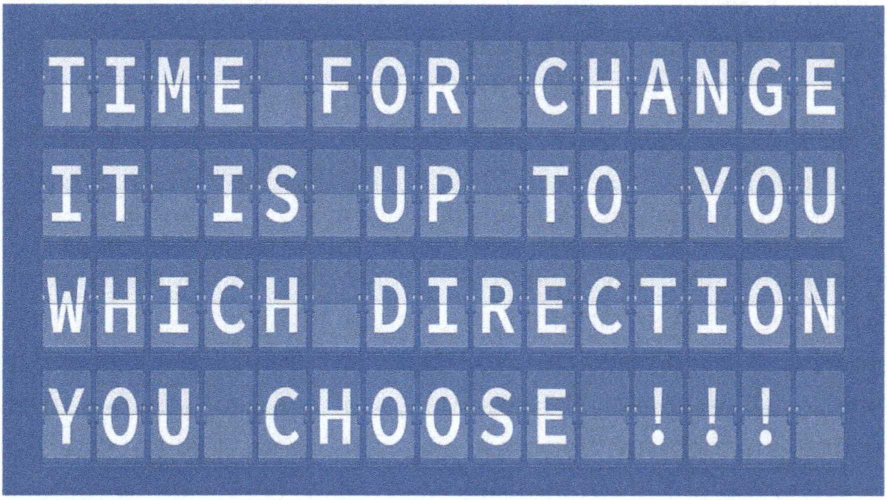

Emotional Response

Emotional responses can be categorized into four basic groups: instrumental, reactive, adaptive, and maladaptive.

Instrumental emotional responses, which can be manipulative, refers to the reactions we express once we've learned that our own emotions (positive or negative) affect other people. For example, someone might express emotions in an attempt to get a person to approve of him or her, do something for him or her, or approve of him or her. These responses can be deliberate and conscious, but they can also be learned in childhood, and expressed without a conscious effort to do so. Instrumental emotional responses can correlate to a person's shame (for example, artificial embarrassment), fear (for example, crying wolf), anger (for example, bullying), or sadness (for example, crocodile tears). Instrumental emotional responses can be quite manipulative in nature; moreover, their function is to use interpersonal dynamics for personal gain.

Reactive emotional responses refer to emotions that are expressed after an original emotion is expressed. The primary emotional response can escalate to create the secondary emotional response. For example, you can feel anxious about feeling anxious, or you can feel sad about feeling sad. The reactive, secondary emotions can also serve as a defense mechanism to cope with the primary emotional response. For example, you can feel fear to avoid your feelings of anger or sadness. Reactive emotional responses occur as a defense, because experiencing the deeper emotions can be more painful and difficult to process.

Adaptive emotional responses are healthy, appropriate, and beneficial. For example, if you experience a loss, feeling sadness would be an adaptive emotional response. The sadness is healthy. Likewise, fear is a healthy emotional response to a threat. It's motivation to avoid the threat and stay safe.

Maladaptive emotional responses are unhealthy and dysfunctional responses. Typically, they stem from emotions from the past - sometimes a traumatic event. The emotional response isn't appropriate because it does not align with the current circumstances; rather, it's a conditioned and unhealthy response that is expressed without deliberate effort.

Appropriate and Inappropriate Emotional Responses

Young children typically identify just a few emotions (for example, sad, happy, and angry). As adults, though, were equipped with the ability to recognize and express a vast array of emotions. When things happen in life, we all experience emotional responses; however, the way we react to them can impact the circumstances. For example, reacting negatively or inappropriately can exacerbate a situation and make matters worse.

As an example, assume that your ex has asked your best friend out for a date. This might cause you to feel a whole host of different emotions, including confusion, jealousy, and anger. These are all valid and normal emotional responses.

Now, you can react to that emotional response in a few different ways. Do you:

a. completely isolate yourself, end all communication with your friend, avoid him or her, and stew in your own emotions without dealing with them?

b. plot revenge, spread lies about your friend, lash out at him or her, ridicule him or her, and shut him or her out of group activities?

c. adjust your focus onto yourself, engage in self- care, spend time with another friend, and exercise?

The first two options, even though they might seem tempting, would likely cause more issues in the long term. The third choice might not provide immediate satisfaction, but it's the most healthy option. It would facilitate your journey toward positively managing disappointment and dealing with life's problems.

It can help to evaluate how you're feeling before you react. Your impulse might be to kick and scream out of frustration, but it won't help you in either the short term or long term. The goal is to achieve success in life, and that includes reacting in an appropriate fashion

The Head vs. The Heart

Some might argue that responding emotionally (and reacting to one's emotions) is inappropriate and inefficient. Ignoring either logic or emotions can lead to shortsighted decisions, though. We do make logical choices, but even when it doesn't seem apparent, emotion plays a role as well. Emotional intelligence involves having the head and the heart collaborate. If you pair logic with emotions, you essentially have a balance that includes the best of both worlds.

Chapter 17: Reading Emotions and Body Language

Not everyone will openly announce what he or she is feeling. How can you tell if someone is angry or sad if that person doesn't come right out and tell you? Facial expressions and body language can tell you a lot about what a person is thinking and feeling. Emotional intelligence includes empathy, and that requires being able to recognize others' feelings ... even if he or she doesn't tell you what they are.

Facial Expressions

Nonverbal behavior helps us "read" people. Typical facial expressions can be faked, though. (Have you ever puta smile on your face even though you felt absolutely terrible?) It's important to be able to understand microexpressions, which are completely involuntary. The duration is generally very brief and understanding what it means will help you better understand people.

There are seven basic micro-expressions:

- anger
- contempt
- disgust
- fear
- happiness
- sadness
- surprise

A micro-expression can come and go in a fraction of a second, so if you're not paying careful attention, you'll miss it.

We, as humans, all make the same microexpressions. People from various locations and cultures, and even those who were born without eyesight, all make the same facial expressions. It is important to understand the basic microexpressions, and it can be helpful to practice in a mirror.

Anger

As part of an anger microexpressions, a person's eyes will lower and seem to squint a bit, fixed in a hard stare. You'll notice small vertical lines between his or her eyebrows. Lips are typically tightly together, possibly with the outside corners downturned. You'll see nostrils flare a bit and the jaw will protrude.

Contempt

For a contempt micro-expression, you'll notice asymmetry in a person's mouth. One side will be raised, while the other will not be.

Disgust

With a disgust micro-expression, you'll notice that a few facial features rise. A person's cheeks, lower lip, and upper eyelid will be raised. Additionally, you'll see wrinkle lines on and around the nose, and beneath the lower eyelid.

Fear

For a fear micro-expression, a person's eyebrows will be raised, and they'll look more horizontal than usual. You'll notice wrinkles between his or her eyebrows, and the sclera will be visible above the iris (but not below). His or her upper eyelid will be raised (but not the lower eyelid). A person's mouth is typically open, with lips slightly stretched back.

Happiness

A happiness micro-expression is the one that is easiest to try to feign. A person's mouth may or may not be open, but the corners are upturned, with a wrinkle that spans from the outside of the nose to the outer lip. His or her cheeks will rise. You'll notice small wrinkles ("crow's feet") near the outside corners of his or her eyes. You might also see wrinkles near the person's lower eyelid.

Sadness

With a sadness micro-expression, you'll notice that a person's lower lip protrudes into a pout. His or her jaw will come up, and the lips' corners will be downturned.

The eyebrows' inner corners will be pulled in and up, creating skin bunching. Incidentally, a sadness micro- expression is the most difficult one to try to fake.

Surprise

The surprise micro-expression includes raised, curved eyebrows. You'll see lateral wrinkles appear across the forehead. A person's jaw will typically drop a bit, parting his or her teeth, but in a relaxed fashion. His or her eyes will be wide open, making the sclera visible above and below the iris.

Body Language

Being in tune with others' emotions is an integral part of emotional intelligence, and the ability to read nonverbal cues really gives you an advantage as a leader. Unfortunately, a lot of people try to mask their feelings, and do their best to keep their faces from showing everything. Micro-expressions are a valuable tool in understanding nonverbal communication, but they can be easy to miss, since they happen so quickly. Luckily, body language speaks volumes. Learning to evaluate what a person's body is telling you is quite a valuable skill.

The Eyes

A person's eyes can tell you a lot. Pay close attention to the amount of eye contact someone makes with you. Looking away can reflect apathy or deceit, while looking at the floor can indicate that he or she is shy, nervous, or intimidated.

Look at a person's pupils, if you're close enough. Dilation is an involuntary movement that can occur for numerous reasons. When a person is concentrating on a person or thing he or she likes, pupils will dilate. It's a way to determine if someone is having a favorable reaction to you and his or her interaction with you.

If someone's blinking quickens, it could indicate that there's something going on. The rate of a person's blinking will accelerate if he or she is feeling stressed or overwhelmed. Additionally, if increased blinking rate is coupled with touching one's face, there could be underlying deceit.

Everyone occasionally glances at other people and things, even during a conversation. Peeking at something can indicate that a person desires it. For instance, glancing at an exit door might suggest that someone wants to leave.

The Mouth

A person's mouth can convey various nonverbal communication. Smiling is a gesture that can be done in different ways. A real, genuine smile involves a person's entire face. It shows that a person is happy and comfortable in the environment. A fake smile, in contrast, only engages the person's mouth. It typically indicates that a person wants to show approval but is feeling differently in reality. If a person shows a half smile, you'll see only one side of his or her mouth move. It generally suggests that he or she is uncertain (or utilizing sarcasm).

A grimace is different than a smile. Typically, it means that a person isn't satisfied; when it's quickly replaced by a fake smile, it means that he or she is trying to hide that. Purses lips that are tightly drawn also suggest disapproval; in contrast, a relaxed mouth generally reflects a favorable mood.

If someone touches his or her mouth while speaking, it can be an indication that he or she is not being completely honest.

Distance

How far is a person from you while the two of you are communicating? The distance is known as proximity, and it can say a lot about how someone is feeling. Someone who feels that he or she has a positive rapport with you is likely to sit or stand in close proximity. If a person backs away from you, this likely suggests the opposite. Remember that cultural differences can account for varied preferences with personal space, so distance isn't a perfect measure of whether or not someone is responding well to you.

Mirroring

Does the other person mimic your body language? This is known as mirroring. Someone can mirror your body language by adjusting his or her posture to match yours, crossing his or her legs to look like yours, or resting his or her hands the same way you do. If someone mirrors your body language, it's a signal that he or she istrying to make a connection.

Head Movement

Many people nod during conversations, to show that they're listening. If someone nods slowly, it means that he or she is engaged in the dialogue and would like you to continue speaking. If someone nods quickly, though, it suggests that he or she is ready for you to wrap itup. That person either wants a chance to speak or wants the conversation to conclude.

A head tilt to the side during a conversation can mean

that a person is interested in what you're saying. If he or she tilts it back, though, it can indicate skepticism or uncertainty. As mentioned above, people often look at people and things that interest them. It's essentially pointing but using a face instead of a finger. In a meeting, people typically face the leaders.

Hands and Feet

You might not think to look at a person's feet, but they can be very telling with nonverbal cues. If a person concentrates on his or her facial expressions and posture, it's easy to forget about the feet. They can reveal quite a bit about what someone is thinking and feeling. Generally, a person will subconsciously point his or her feet in the direction they'd like to go. If someone has his or her feet pointed toward you, it can mean that you are well received. In contrast, a person could be involved in a conversation with you but have his or her feet pointed elsewhere (toward a door, another person, etc.). This likely suggests that he or she would rather be somewhere else.

Hands also offer nonverbal cues when we look at body language. Hand placement, such as in pockets or on his or her head, can mean a person is anxious or deceitful. It's also important to pay attention to a person's hand gestures. A person will point or gesticulate in the direction of someone whom he or she likes. If someone is sitting at a table and rests his or her head on a hand supported by an elbow on the table can indicate two very different things - boredom or focus. In cases like that, it's best to look for additional nonverbal cues.

If someone holds an object between himself or herself and you, it's a symbolic barrier. It signifies a blockade. Crossed arms can mean a number of different things, such as:

- vulnerability
- defensiveness
- anxiety
- confidence (when coupled with a genuine smile and relaxed posture)

Additionally, if you're speaking to someone and he or she stands akimbo, it's a nonverbal exertion of dominance. It generally reads as aggressive.

With all body language and facial expressions, context is key. Keep in mind that not every technique will applyto every person. To be emotionally intelligent, it's essential that you take all factors into consideration.

Chapter 18: Leader Competencies

Leadership comes in many different forms. We see leaders in politics, the military, and business. At its core, leadership means devising a plan to guide a team to victory. It involves establishing direction, constructing and sharing a clear vision, and inspiring others to join in the quest. Leadership always requires efficient management skills.

Constructing a Vision

A vision is more than just the picture that an individual has in his or her mind to depict success. It provides a finish line of sorts, that indicatesthe achievement of set goals. A vision must be realistic, but it's also utilized to inspire others and convince them that the goal is worthwhile. It sets the tone and makes priorities clear for anyone involved. A vision means that you're not quite satisfied with the status quo; you're proactively looking ahead.

It's a leader's job to make his or her vision fascinating, appealing, and convincing. The goal is to compel others by having them embrace your vision. As a leader, you'll inspire people by supplying them with a vivid picture of how the future will look once your objectives have been met. It's important to appeal to people in a way that makes your vision relatable to them.

Inspiration and Motivation

A vision is the essential start, but it will only get you so far. The next step in leadership is inspiring and motivating a team of people to work together to achieve a common goal: actualizing your vision.

Just as it gets challenging to motivate yourself once the novelty has worn off, motivating others also gets difficult over time. Enthusiasm fades. An effective leader anticipates this, and diligently works to continue the encouragement throughout the duration of the project. You'll need to continue to find ways to connect with your team, keep your vision at the forefront of their minds, and inspire them to keep pushing.

You can appeal to people's motivation in different ways. Efficient and effective leaders utilize both intrinsic and extrinsic motivators. For example, take a look at the following chain reaction:

hard work ➡ *positive results* ➡ *reward*

Hard work yields positive results, which then produce a reward. This mentality appeal to team members' internal motivation (wanting to do a good job) and external motivation (wanting a reward).

Leaders often have power of some sort. For example, you might be in a position to issue paychecks or assign personnel changes. A good leader doesn't rely too heavily on these things when he or she is working to motivate others.

Management of the Vision

Part of your leadership role obviously entails management, but you're not merely managing people. For a goal to be successfully achieved, actualizing the vision requires work, and it needs to be managed. In order to achieve this, specific goals need to be set.

Any member of a team that is working on delivering your vision will need clear performance goals. These goals must correlate to your vision. You must also efficiently manage any change that is necessary, so that things run smoothly for everyone involved.

Coaching and Teamwork

As a leader, you're the coach of your team. Your job is not just to supervise; rather, you must make sure that everyone is equipped with the skills and strategies that are needed to fulfill your vision. A team dynamic means that development and training are key. Ensuring that all team members are fully capable happens through coaching, assessment, and feedback.

A leader always looks for leadership potential in members of his or her team. If you develop these skills in-house, you're creating sustainability, and the success of your team will continue into the future.

Leadership Skills

Leaders should always concern themselves with building the necessary competencies to be successful. There are numerous valuable skills involved in leadership, let's explore six of them.

1. Emotional intelligence is, as we know, to be in tune with your emotions and the emotions of others. A leader must be able to accurately read emotional situations and communicate with other people in a way that incorporates emotions. Building emotional intelligence involves practice. First, you can practice appropriately expressing and regulating your own emotions. You can also practice evaluating others' nonverbal communication. It's also important to expose yourself to different people and social environments so that you can practice engaging others and developing your perception. Put your listening skills to use and hone your communication abilities. Look at situations from the perspective of others.

2. Conflict management skills are absolutely essential for a leader. When others are in disagreement, a leader can be called upon to mediate. An effective leader is able to successfully resolve these conflicts. It's also essential that you're able to resolve (or, better yet, avoid) your own conflicts. It's important to be able to generate solutions that are either a compromise or a win- win cooperation.

3. Decision making is a skill that is essential for a leader. It entails making good choices and also leading the process of making good choices. A successful leader knows when it's an appropriate time to make a decision. Additionally, he or she knows when to consult others or hand the responsibility to someone else. The best way to practice effective decision making is to learn from your mistakes. It's helpful to keep a mental inventory of what was involved in decisions you've made in the past, and whether or not the outcome was a success.
4. A successful leader has fortitude. It's necessary to have courage when you're taking risks, even when they're based on reliable information. Having fortitude means that you're not afraid to stand up for what's right. Developing fortitude involves supporting your team and standing by your principles.

5. Good judgment is necessary for successful leadership. When you're able to open your mind to others' perspectives and consider different points of view, you make prudent decisions. Practicing good judgment means that you ask questions, consider other people's opinions, and understand the scope of your actions.

6. Of course, a successful leader needs to be competent in his or her area of expertise. While this was once the most important trait of a leader, we now know that the best leader for a team might not be the one with the most technical knowledge. It is important, though, for a leader to build his or her industry expertise and realize that development is a long-term process. Successful leaders take every opportunity to learn as much as they can. This can happen through getting to know team members, studying the competition, and educating yourself.

Chapter 19: The Ideal Leader

Leadership comes in many forms, but there are some attributes that are universal for successful leaders. Among others, these abilities include delegation, communication, and positive attitude. A great leader engages his or her team members, exhibits innovative problem solving, and inspires other people.

To be the ideal leader, though, there is one characteristic that you must possess: the love of learning and the desire to keep doing it.

It's always optimal to have a leader who asks questions and would never insult anyone by assuming that he or she knows everything. As an ideal leader, you can't be scared about taking missteps; a mistake is only a mistake if you don't learn a lesson from it. A highly successful leader will ask for constructive criticism, genuinely listen to feedback, and implement changes for future improvement.

Maybe you feel as though you've learned everything there is to know about your industry. Especially if you've been doing it for a long time, it can start to feel as if there isn't anything you haven't already mastered. If this is the case, how can you enhance your knowledge or increase your understanding?

Even the most educated of us never stop learning, because none of us knows what the future holds. Circumstances, technology, and other relevant factors change every single day, and no amount of planning serves as a guarantee. The ideal leader must be open- minded when it comes to the concept of change. Being open to change will make navigating unfamiliar territory easier and more comfortable. In addition to being open to change, you must also be open to learning. New ideas and concepts will be easier to adopt if you keep an open mind.

In our ever-changing world, your skill set needs to evolve over time. Adjusting perspective will help you stay aligned with your clients' or customers' needs. It is imperative that you stay relevant. Updating skills and renewing your understanding will keep you from falling behind. Especially for millennials, conventional methods of training (i.e. the classroom) are simply not enough. For the younger half of the workforce who grew up with access to seemingly unlimited technological resources, the concept of always learning more comes pretty naturally.

Many people express interest in continuing their learning, but unfortunately, a lot of organizations are not prepared to fulfill this need. It's important that organizations collaborate to offer training and continued education using innovative, efficient methods. It is in everyone's best interest to equip team members with the skills they will need to develop into ideal leaders. This includes long-term goals outside the realm of technical industry know-how. It's just as important for a successful leader to be adept with building relationships, researching information, and sharing knowledge. It's worthwhile for an effective leader to incorporate a shift in the organization's culture, utilizing the vast resources available through technology.

Learning is not a checklist or a straight path withclearly defined start and finish lines. Learning is a journey that will take you places you might not have expected. If you're open to learning, you'll be able to competently handle anything that comes your way.

Discovering information should be very simple, considering the immediate and constant access we have. When you're seeking knowledge, though, it's imperative that you ensure the data is applicable, accurate, and relevant. Always use reputable sources. Read critically. You only want information that is legitimate, and it can take time to sift through all the content that doesn't apply. You want a variety of trusted sources that can offer new perspectives and facilitate your informed decision making.

Applying the new information in an effective way is what will transform you from a good leader into the ideal leader. Learning and critical thinking will help you find genuine meaning in your feelings, thoughts, and experiences. Once you've learned something new and tweaked it to align with your needs, the next (very big) step is to implement that information.

It's always important to "pay it forward" when you learn new things. Information has been shared with you, so it makes sense that you should also pass it along. Sometimes, this happens organically, and you'll find yourself relaying new information through regular conversation. Other times, though, it will need to be more of a deliberate effort. It's essential that you're frequently exchanging information, ideas, resources, and experiences with your peers, colleagues, and team members. The entire organization will benefit from interpersonal collaboration. Collective learning is valuable for everyone involved, and it will make each person feel like a leader who has facilitated others' development as well as his or her own.

It's important to remember that you needn't give orders to be a leader. Anyone in an organization can be an ideal leader, regardless of rank or position. Effective and successful leadership does not come from commanding others; rather, the ideal leader is the person who decides time, effort, and energy to continuous learning. The motivation to keep learning, and the love of doing so, is what separates ordinary leaders from extraordinary leaders. Education comes in many forms, and the ideal leader incorporates a variety of them because he or she sees his or her journey as a never-ending quest.

Chapter 20: Behavioral Communication

Behavior

Behavior refers to our actions and mannerisms; it's used to describe how we conduct ourselves. Typically, it applies to how we present ourselves to others.

Behavioral Communication

Behavioral communication comprises the various ways people express themselves (specifically, their thoughts, feelings, desires, and needs) in lieu of open and direct statements. This includes nonverbal communication, of course, but behavioral communication includes more than facial expression, posture, and hand placement. It's the tendency that some have to send indirect messages to others.

Any behavior can be communication, if that person intended to send a message of some sort. For example, a person's tattoos might express the message that he or she is creative and unique. Additionally, a lack of behavior can be considered a behavior. For instance, not picking your wife up from the airport (after you'd promised to) could convey the message that she's not a priority.

Everyone communicates differently, and the same is true for behavioral communication. Your communication (both verbal and nonverbal) is substantially affected by your style of behavior. With the self-awareness you've developed as part of your emotional intelligence, you should be able to recognize your own behavioral style.

Types of Behavioral Communication

There are four fundamental types of behavioral communication:

aggressive
assertive
passive

passive-aggressive

Aggressive Behavioral Communication

When someone's behavioral communication is aggressive, it means that he or she exhibits sudden angry actions that reflect intentions of hurting another person or a thing. This type of communication generates (usually unnecessary) conflict, and it typically includes insults and personal attacks. Aggressive behavioral communication is intimidating and controlling in nature, and they stem from a person's insecurities, lack of empathy, and selfishness. This form of communication comes from a very closed mindset, and the aggressor is not interested in listening to your perspective.

Some (but not all) of the behaviors you'll see conveyed through aggressive communication include:

- exhibiting stiff posture
- frowning
- glaring
- ignoring others
- insulting others
- intimidating others
- not considering others' thoughts and feelings
- not listening to others
- speaking in a condescending fashion
- speaking loudly and quickly

For those involved in this form of behavioral communication, emotions can vary. The aggressor generally feels angry, impatient, and frustrated. The person on the receiving end of this behavior feels hurt, humiliated, fearful, and defensive. Unfortunately, aggressive behavioral communication typically results in escalation. Counter-aggression is quite common.

Aside from in urgent situations, aggressive communication isn't usually appropriate. It's problematic at best; it certainly doesn't encourage open communication. It can be unsafe, as well, because flared tempers can lead to physical altercations.

Assertive Behavioral Communication

To be assertive is to appropriately and directly convey your own thoughts and emotions. Assertive behavioral communication is predicated on the idea that you are solely responsible for expressing yourself. If you want to resolve an issue with someone, it's up to you to clearly communicate with him or her what you need. This form of communication is respectful to all parties; the person on the receiving end can expect to have his or her thoughts and emotions considered.

Being assertive means that you're being direct, but not combative. It helps to avoid conflicts before they arise, form and maintain healthy relationships, and foster open dialogue. Unfortunately, this win-win type of communication is the least used of the four.

A successful leader with high emotional intelligence assertively communicates; he or she is open to new perspectives and opinions. High self-esteem helps an assertive communicator listen without getting offended, while healthy self-regulation helps him or her set clear expectations. Other essential parts of assertive behavioral communication are active listening and problem-solving skills.

If you are engaged in assertive behavioral communication, you will likely present behaviors such as:

- accepting responsibility
- listening to others' opinions
- presenting upright and relaxed posture
- appropriately responding to others

- taking accountability for mistakes
- setting attainable goals
- showing receptive body language
- openly and clearly expressing emotions
- exhibiting self-control
- treating others as equals
- speaking clearly
- making eye contact
- encouraging others to express themselves

Those who assertively communicates are generally self-confident and self-respecting; additionally, the person on the receiving end typically respects him or her. A communicator who is assertive is believable, and he or she will be clear about expectations.

Assertive behavioral communication is positive for everyone involved. It creates a respectful and peaceful environment where people feel connected. Communicating assertively is necessary in leadership.

Passive Behavioral Communication

In direct contrast, passive communication involves not expressing your thoughts and feelings. It entails putting your own needs and desires on the back burner in order to make everyone else happy. Avoiding conflict is a primary goal of a passive communicator, and he or she will be internally uncomfortable and upset if it means being well-liked by other people.

Passive communication stems from a person's feeling that his or her needs are not a priority; moreover, he or she fears that speaking up will lead to rejection. A passive communicator might be so accustomed to ignoring his or her own needs that he or she doesn't even recognize them anymore. Low self-esteem and the tendency to trust others but not oneself are common for passive communicators.

Someone who exhibits passive behavioral communication will show many characteristics, including:

- avoiding confrontation
- avoiding taking responsibility

- avoiding making decisions
- avoiding eye contact
- referring to others' choices
- speaking softly
- fidgeting
- rejecting compliments
- asking permission
- frequently sighing
- speaking hesitantly

A passive communicator typically feels anxious because there is a constant sense of being powerless and not in control. He or she might also feel resentful that his or her needs are not being considered, even though they are not being expressed. Depressive feelings can come from a sense of hopelessness, and confusion can stem from not understanding his or her own emotions.

Someone on the receiving end of this type of communication can feel very frustrated. In the midst of engaging, the passive communicator will feel anxious, and it can make the other person feel guilty. Generally, a passive communicator will feel resentful or angry afterward.

Unfortunately, passively communicating further erodes a person's self-esteem. This type of communicator will often internalize all the discomfort until it erupts in an unexpected outburst. This then causes feelings of shame, causing a person to continue to communicate passively. It is a cycle that can be difficult to break.

Passive-Aggressive Behavioral Communication

Passive-aggressive behavioral communication combines a few elements of both the passive and aggressive behavioral communication styles. What's unique about this form of communication is that a person will appear to be passive, but indirectly act out his or her underlying anger in other ways. These expressions can include being deliberately inefficient, exaggerating forgetfulness, or procrastinating. Passive-aggressive behavior stems from feelings of resentment and powerlessness.

Passive-aggressive behavioral communication can exhibit various characteristics, including:

- unreliability
- giving backhanded compliments
- gossiping
- making wistful statements
- patronizing
- deliberately ignoring someone
- sulking

- complaining
- muttering to himself or herself
- sabotage
- sarcasm

Many people who communicate in this way also utilize numerous facial expressions, such as a smirk, to express themselves. They might also have a very innocent expression to hide any frustration or anger they're experiencing. Body language is typically awkward and jerky in nature.

Being on the receiving end of passive-aggressive behavior will likely leave you feeling confused and hurt. While it's a frequently used style of communication, it is quite inefficient and ineffective. Passive-aggressive communicators do not address the issue, which means there isn't a chance to resolve it. It's a maladaptive style that results in more passive-aggressive behavior.

Chapter 21:

Positive Communication Style

Robust communication skills are important for any successful leader, and his or her skills greatly influence how an organization grows and develops. A great leader knows that his or her organization's success heavily depends on the leadership's communication skills. He or she must be able to clearly express, and inspire people with, thoughts and ideas. There are numerous factors in strong communication skills, and practicing can enhance your success as a leader. Let's take a look at some of the dynamics of a positive communication style for leaders.

Be an Active Listener

A successful leader knows how to listen before speaking. Making the concerted effort to improve your listening skills will pay off. Some may think that a leader's job is to instruct, direct, and win people over, all through speaking. Using active listening as a strategy, though, is what can make a leader great. Listening to colleagues, clients, and employees will give you insight into their thoughts, needs, and concerns; that information is invaluable to the ideal leader. Getting to know your team members' perspectives will facilitate your role as the coach who guides them to achieve goals. Active listening skills will help you form and maintain relationships, gain understanding, increase efficiency, and solve problems. It's important to take a few moments to listen; your organization's long-term success will benefit from it.

Open Body Language

As discussed in Chapter 17, nonverbal communication is just as important as verbal communication. If your facial expression and body language are inviting and warm, people will tend to be more open with you. They'll be more likely to positively receive your message. Making a conscious effort to improve body language is a part of positive communication that successful leaders remember to do.

It's also important to practice accurately reading others' body language, as they can give you a lot of information through their nonverbal cues. Top leaders know to make eye contact, smile if it's appropriate, refrain from crossing their arms, etc., but they also pay attention to the other person's body language. Sensing how other people feel while you're engaging with them is valuable, and you'll know if you should adjust the conversation accordingly.

Vulnerability

Establishing rapport with others is critical for successful leaders. Forming a connection with others will facilitate your ability to inspire them.

Telling a story of your own might make you feel vulnerable, and that's good. Willingness to share a piece of yourself resonates with people. If you have stories that detail how you've overcome obstacles, sharing them will likely motivate your team members.

Adjusting to Various Communication Styles

It's essential for a leader to be adaptable to a lot of things, and different communication styles are no exception. Knowing your audience goes a long way,and if you take the time to genuinely get to know the members of your team, it will be easy to adjust to their various communication styles. A great leader knows how to take one message and convey it differently to each of his or her team members in ways that will resonate most with them. People are far more likely to want to follow someone with whom they have a connection.

Showing Fairness

A successful leader remembers to be kind and fair when interacting with others. Treating everyone warmly and equally builds trust and helps forge strong relationships. People are far more likely to get on board with your vision if you treat everyone fairly and with respect.

Utilizing Feedback

Great leaders don't just give feedback; they ask for it, as well. Requesting feedback improves communication skills. Implementing changes that reflect that feedback is optimal, and it shows others that you truly value their thoughts and opinions.

When employees communicate concerns, an effective leader will try out possible resolutions to address the issues. It sends the message that all team members are valued, and it keeps communication open.

Giving your team members thoughtful critiques is essential. Overusing praise or being overly critical will cause your words to lose meaning. Offer praise when it's deserved and supply constructive criticism when it's appropriate. Feedback should be positive, and your message will be better received as such. Emphasis on potential improvement or opportunities for growth shows team members that you see their potential.

Engaging and Motivating

A successful leader will engage others while skillfully motivating and inspiring them. Of course, you can appeal to people's needs for things like happiness and success, but an outstanding leader knows that motivation is not one-size-fits-all. If you truly get to know the members of your team, you'll be able to tailor your motivating communication accordingly.

It's a leader's responsibility to inspire his or her team to rally around, embrace your vision, and help achieve a goal. Their motivation for success comes from your inspiration.

Personalize Your Communication

A great leader makes everyone feel important and valuable. Even when a successful leader is speaking to a large group, he or she has the ability to make you feel as though you have a personal connection. It feels as though he or she is speaking directly to you. In your organization, really getting to personally know your team members greatly increases your chances of getting them to support your vision. Even little things, like saying hello and using people's names, can go a long way.

Prioritize

A successful leader knows how valuable everyone's time is. If communication is handled inefficiently, it wastes everybody's time. This inevitably leads to decreased productivity. When you communicate with your team, be direct. Communicate precisely what you want by making the following things very clear:

- goal of the task
- expected duration of task completion
- necessary resources
- relevant details

If this communication is conveyed via email, keep it concise.

Engage in Dialogue

A successful leader avoids talking to his or her team; rather, he or she talks with them. If a leader performs a monologue, team members might not be very receptive, as it can feel as though they're being given commands. In a dialogue, however, they have the opportunity to offer input. It's valuable for you to gain insight into your team and their perspective, so it's best to approach communication in an interactive way.

Clarify Your Communication

An ideal leader's communication is straightforward and

simple. Ambiguity has no place in your expressing what you want from your team. It's imperative that you are precise about expectations. If you need to re-explain, it takes away from time that should be devoted to productivity.

Chapter 22: From Team Member to Great Leader

When an organization has a leadership position to fill, they're faced with a choice: hire from outside, or promote from within. While there are circumstances that require hiring a veteran from outside the company, it's most beneficial to an organization (and its employees) to promote from within. If you're seeking a leadership position in your organization, you can share with management the various reasons that promoting a current team member (you) will benefit everyone.

Hiring from Within

A low turnover rate means that an organization is able to hold onto its best people. Longevity results in a strong, robust company culture. The organization can truly benefit from having a trusted individual in a position of leadership.

Having experience within the organization means that you already know company expectations. You won't require as much of a transition period that a newcomer would. You already have relationships within the company, and more specifically, the team of which you've been a part. Additionally, your promotion would mean that someone else within the organization could move into your current position, thus further fostering the culture of loyalty.

Hiring from outside the company would mean that someone would need to get brought up to speed and create relationships. This can slow down productivity. What's more, it can be a gamble, not knowing what kind of culture a new person will bring into an organization.

Transforming

Once your organization realizes that hiring from within is a valuable investment, you should consider what you need to transform from a team member into a team leader. There are specific ways you can show that you'll be a great fit in a leadership role.

Lead by Example

You don't need an official position as a leader to assume the characteristics of one. Becoming a role model by leading yourself is a great way to showcase your skills. In a culture that demands multi-tasking, it's imperative that you have sharp time management skills. Showing that you can balance tasks (and your personal life) will make you a standout candidate. Managing things like emails, meeting requests, and phone calls (without allowing anything to fall through the cracks) speaks volumes.

Problem Solve and Make Decisions

Being a good problem solver as a team member makes you an incredibly valuable employee. Your strong problem-solving skills will translate well into a leadership role, because even though the problems are different, your skillful strategies for tackling them will still apply.

In addition to problem solving, a successful leader has solid decision-making skills. If there's a specific position to which you'd like to be promoted, you should learn about the decisions that are involved in that role. The ability and desire to learn will not go unnoticed. Having skills is obviously beneficial, but successful leaders having the ability to adeptly acquire new skills.

Market Yourself

If you're interested in being promoted to a leadership position, you'll need to market yourself. The best way to do this is to tap into your emotional intelligence. Your self-awareness will help you understand who you are, what you do best, and what your goals are. Once you know these things, you can present yourself as an attractive candidate for the specific positions your looking for.

Team Leading

The leader of a team or department can sometimes have difficulty finding balance between formal leadership and contributing team member. It's essential to have the ability to use both perspectives. Leading a team also requires delegation, boundaries, and trust - all things that fall under the umbrella of emotional intelligence.

People Skills

Remember that a leader doesn't lead a department or an organization; he or she leads people. Regardless of your industry, you're in the people business. Success comes from teamwork and communication.

If your goal is to rise in the ranks, show that your communication skills are top notch. Show that you have a clear understanding of what success looks like for you.

Be present, attentive, and engaged in meetings. Practice your active listening skills. Use positive body language and assertive behavioral communication. Provide constructive feedback that will help improve productivity. Facilitate problem solving and conflict resolution among your teammates. Get to know your fellow team members so that you can motivate and inspire them.

Delegating is a skill that a lot of leaders have trouble mastering in the beginning. The goal is to delegate problems, not solutions, to your team. When you are given tasks as a member of the team, do your best to complete them efficiently. Show that you recognize that the delegation comes with trust in you and your skills. As a leader, you'll be the one breaking down large jobs into manageable chunks for your team to work on. You'll show your team that you have confidence in them by clearly stating expectations but not micromanaging.

It's also necessary to manage inevitable change and its effect on your team and organization. Transition can be quite difficult for a lot of people, and a leader guides the team through the process.

Strategies

Of course, technical expertise in your industry is essential for team members and leaders alike. In addition to the know-how, though, strategizing skills are very important.

If you look at the big picture, your organization has a grand vision of how it will reach its goals and find success. What role does your department or team play in that vision? How can you divide the long-term goal into projects and benchmarks for your team? A successful leader doesn't blindly begin to work on a project; rather, he or she has strategies to implement.

Overall, a successful leader manages the organization's vision. It's a leader's job to develop a precise vision for what the organization will do to improve its customers' lives. Additionally, a successful leader communicates that vision to the team that will bring it to life. As a team member, showcase your ability to implement effective strategies to see the organization's vision come to fruition.

Chapter 23: Mistakes Leaders Make

Leadership comes with various responsibilities. It can be a bit overwhelming, especially being held to high expectations by yourself and others. Managing a team, and issues in the workplace, can be a lot to juggle. As humans, we sometimes make mistakes. It's natural. It's important to remember that mistakes are learning opportunities that facilitate growth. Fixing common mistakes is beneficial to you as the leader and to your team. Let's discuss some typical leadership mistakes and how to avoid them.

Failure to Delegate

When you've been promoted to a leadership position, it's generally because you excel in knowing what needs to be done and delivering results. Some of us are taught to do it ourselves if we want something done correctly, but that mindset is a mistake for a leader.

It's important for your team to know that you expect tasks to be fully completed. If team members knowthat you'll likely swoop in and tweak it anyway, they'll reduce their effort. You want your team to work to their full potential, and it's obviously silly to create extra work for yourself. Delegation is key.

Work alongside your team and guide them through their work, but don't do it for them. They need to know that you trust them and have confidence in their abilities. They will not feel challenged if you're doing their work for them.

Believing that you're the only one who could possibly complete tasks properly will result in bottlenecked productivity, and you'll end up under extra, unnecessary stress. Delegation of tasks allows you to tend to the bigger picture for which you are responsible.

Neglecting to Provide Feedback

Not providing your team members with clear and prompt feedback is doing them a disservice, as it denies them the opportunity to grow and improve. It's a very common mistake that leaders make, unfortunately. If you wait until a performance review to broach the subject of an issue that needs to be remedied, in the meantime, that team member will continue to make the mistake. It will become a habit, and your bringing it up at an annual review will likely come as a surprise. Feedback is a powerful tool if it's utilized effectively, and everyone (your team members, the organization as a whole, and you) deserve to have things run smoothly. Continuous feedback allows for clear expectations for everyone.

Avoiding Conflict

Issues and disagreements are natural, and they'll inevitably come up. A successful leader handles them fairly, maintaining a balanced climate. Sometimes, conflict is avoidable, but completely avoiding confrontation is a mistake. Ignoring issues with performance or personality disputes can lead to resentment and bottled-up emotions that tend to erupt. It's best to set the tone that situations are addressedas they happen.

Remember that a successful leader is emotionally intelligent. Your empathy and social skills will allow you to recognize how others are feeling. Your team members will know that being open is safe and expected. Your motivation to maintain successful productivity will encourage you to mediate, communicate openly, and lead by example.

Failing to Set Goals and Define Vision

A company progresses because it has a vision. It's necessary for focus with tasks and projects, proper resource planning, and accurate metrics. The vision keeps the organization in alignment, cooperating to reach common goals. Without a clear vision, your team will lack focus and direction.

Without goals, your team can't be productive. Everyone needs to clearly understand what his or her work means, and what the end result will be. If you don't set goals (and monitor the progress), it will be impossible for your team to properly prioritize. Make sure everyone involved explicitly understands the vision, goals, timeframe, and resources.

Reactivity Instead of Proactivity

Changes happen in every industry. Without change, organizations would stagnate and fail. While adjusting to developments can sometimes be difficult, a leader must confront the changes and recognize how they will impact your organization. If you, as a leader, wait for transformations to be underway before you react to them, you're too late.

Be proactive. Be honest with your team members. Translations can be stressful, and it's your responsibility to alleviate the pressure that your team feels. Ensure that your team is ready for transitions by training team members on new skills, updating relevant resources, and renewing certifications.

Forgetting Humility

A role in leadership can feed a person's ego if he or she feels a sense of power. It's a mistake to start to feel irreproachable or infallible; furthermore, it will alienate your team members.

A successful leader remains humble. Your team needs to know that you have shortcomings, and that you're comfortable with them. It's perfectly natural to make mistakes, and your team will feel more comfortable, confident, and open-minded knowing that it's okay. Learning from mistakes and understanding the value of the lessons that come from them, makes us wiser and more capable.

Misunderstanding Motivation

A successful leader needs to know his or her team members well; part of that includes understanding what motivates them. It's a mistake to assume that everyone is motivated solely by a paycheck. Monetary rewards are great, but it's likely that your team is motivated by more than that.

Some of your team members might be motivated by the satisfaction of a job well done. Others might be motivated by things like added responsibility, verbal praise, or being able to take their families on vacation. Be mindful of people's general desire to maintain a balance between work and home; it's common nowadays for team members to find flexibility very motivating.

Misunderstanding Your Position

Upon becoming a manager or a leader, you'll realize that your responsibilities change. It can be easy to lose sight of this, though, if you're now leading a team of which you were once a part. You've been hired to lead, which requires a different skill set, and many leaders lose sight of that in the beginning. Your technical skills are only half of the equation; remember that you need to implement your leadership skills in order to be successful with your new set of responsibilities.

Losing Faith in Your Abilities

Some leaders constantly second-guess themselves, and it's a mistake that can have devastating consequences. Remember that you were hired into a leadership position because at least one other person has confidence in your judgment. If you're not listening to your gut, and you're always doubting yourself, the confidence will quickly erode. Trust yourself and your instincts. Don't forget that you were chosen to lead a team for a reason.

Forgetting That You're a Team

As a leader, it's very easy to get caught up in your own tasks and general workload, but don't make the mistake of being unavailable to your team. Your projects are important, but your people are your priority. They need your guidance and support in order to reach the goals you've set for them. If you need to, designate time to spend time with your team. Utilize your active listening skills and let your team members tell you what they need.

Of course, you want to avoid micromanaging your team, but don't make the mistake of going too far in the other direction. A balanced approach is ideal, and at the end of the day, your team members need to know they can depend on being able to talk to you.

Be a role model by setting a good example. Don't expect your team to do anything that you're not also willing to do. Keep a positive attitude, follow your organization's policies, and be a team player. You have people looking to you to walk the walk.

Conclusion

The term "emotional intelligence" is something that has been around for decades, but some people can still be a bit confused by what it means. The five basic components of emotional intelligence – self-awareness, self-regulation, motivation, empathy, and social skills – work in concert. Emotional intelligence is your capacity to understand and express your emotions and also manage interpersonal relationships, but it's also the key to achieving success in your personal and professional lives. Your emotional quotient (EQ) is just as important as your intelligence quotient (IQ), and increasing your emotional intelligence will enhance your success. Of all the factors that impact your potential as a leader, your emotional intelligence is the most important.

Understanding your own emotions (and, therefore, the emotions of others) helps you develop the empathy that is necessary for successful leadership. Active listening skills, and the ability to clearly read nonverbal communication, will afford you the opportunity to truly get to know your team members. Understanding the people on your team, showing them respect, and listening to their questions and concerns will foster an environment of open communication for everyone.

As the leader, you have a vision, and it's your job to motivate your team to achieve the goals that align with it. The only way this is possible is if you've developed your emotional intelligence and you have robust social skills, empathy, motivation.

There are numerous leadership competencies, and also common mistakes that should be avoided. Successful leadership is complex; if it were simple, everyone would make a great leader. Practicing the tenets of emotional intelligence (such as positive body language, assertive behavioral communication, empathy, and active listening skills) are surefire ways to develop top-notch leadership skills. Successful leaders know that integrating these skills into their professional lives benefits everyone involved. If you're ready to lead, motivate others, and inspire a team to work together to achieve goals, *Emotional Intelligence for Leadership* is a resource you can (and should) revisit as needed.

CPSIA information can be obtained
at www.ICGtesting.com
Printed in the USA
BVHW062041010321
601387BV00007B/350

9 781914 136290